Praise for *Not Drinking Tonight*

"*Not Drinking Tonight* is the book for anyone questioning their relationship with alcohol or other addictive behaviors. I love how this book pushes us to examine what we've been taught about alcohol, how it's impacting us, and what we can do about it. This guide will help anyone who's ever felt stuck in their drinking habits, without slapping on scary labels or prescribing full sobriety."
—Whitney Goodman, LMFT

"*Not Drinking Tonight* is a wonderful guide to setting healthy boundaries with alcohol—and yourself. Amanda helps you dig into the root of your struggles to better understand why you drink and why you might want to stop—setting you up for a more fulfilling life all around, even if you don't choose full sobriety. Readers will gain the self-awareness, compassion, and confidence to make choices that better serve them."

—Nedra Tawwab, MSW, LCSW, *New York Times* bestselling author of *Set Boundaries, Find Peace*

"A knowledgeable, compassionate, and supportive guide. With a wealth of examples, tools, practices, and new ways of relating to both alcohol and the self, *Not Drinking Tonight* will be an accessible and revelatory balm for anyone questioning the kind of life they want to create outside of drinking."

—Lisa Olivera, LMFT, founder of @lisaolivera and author of *Already Enough*

"I truly believe that anyone will benefit from reading this book, regardless of their relationship with alcohol. This book is such a great, relatable resource that will help us cultivate more self-awareness and compassion while gently examining our relationship with alcohol, and ourselves."

—Caroline Dooner, author of the bestselling book *The F*ck It Diet*

"In this gentle, forthright, and actionable book, Amanda White busts the myth that we need to be at rock bottom to ask for help. She challenges us to heal beyond the label we tie to our struggles and creates space for us to shed layers of shame, which keep us shackled to narratives of low self-worth. Whether you're newly sober, not-yet-sober, toying with the idea of sobriety, or never even contemplated a life beyond sobriety until this very moment, this book has gems of wisdom to offer you on your journey."

—Jennifer R. Wolkin, PhD (Dr. Jen), neuropsychologist and author of *Quick Calm: Easy Meditations to Short-Circuit Stress Using Mindfulness and Neuroscience*

"As a therapist, this is the book about drinking I have been waiting for. *Not Drinking Tonight* offers a fresh perspective on substance misuse and gently guides you, with relatable examples, how to choose to stop drinking tonight, tomorrow, and—if you want—forever. Finally, a book on drinking that I truly believe in and am excited to recommend to my clients."

—Elizabeth Earnshaw, LMFT, relationship expert, founder of @lizlistens, and author of *I Want This to Work*

"Written in a smart, relatable style, and rooted in actual therapeutic expertise, *Not Drinking Tonight* is the self-help resource manual that we need. Amanda walks readers through a journey of gaining a deeper understanding of their relationship to alcohol, regardless of addiction status. I especially appreciated the education provided around trauma and reparenting. Amanda's book is a resource that I know I will use for both myself and my clients for years to come—an absolute gift."

—Dr. Colleen Reichmann, clinical psychologist and author of *The Inside Scoop on Eating Disorder Recovery*

"*Not Drinking Tonight* is an of-the-moment book that brings the #quitlit genre to the next level. White's writing about mental health and sobriety is just as helpful and accessible as her popular Instagram account."

—Tawny Lara, sober sex and relationships writer

Not
Drinking
Tonight

Not Drinking Tonight

A Guide to Creating
a Sober Life You Love

Amanda E. White

hachette
BOOKS

New York

Hachette Go, an imprint of Hachette Books
Hachette Book Group
1290 Avenue of the Americas
New York, NY 10104
HachetteGo.com
Facebook.com/HachetteGo
Instagram.com/HachetteGo

First Edition: January 2022

Hachette Books is a division of Hachette Book Group, Inc.
The Hachette Go and Hachette Books name and logos are trademarks of Hachette Book Group, Inc.

The publisher is not responsible for websites (or their content) that are not owned by the publisher.

Print book interior design by Amy Quinn.

Library of Congress Cataloging-in-Publication Data

Names: White, Amanda, author.
Title: Not drinking tonight : a guide to creating a sober life you love / Amanda White.
Description: First edition. | New York : Hachette Go, 2022. | Includes bibliographical references and index.
Identifiers: LCCN 2021036037 | ISBN 9780306925856 (hardcover) | ISBN 9780306925863 (ebook)
Subjects: LCSH: Women alcoholics--Social conditions. | Women alcoholics--Psychology. | Women--Alcohol use. | Temperance.
Classification: LCC HV5137 .W55 2022 | DDC 362.292082--dc23
LC record available at https://lccn.loc.gov/2021036037

ISBNs: 9780306925856 (paper over board); 9780306925863 (ebook)

Printed in the United States of America

LSC-C

Printing 2, 2022

This book is dedicated to my parents, who never gave up on me even when I wanted to give up on myself.

Contents

Introduction

"I'm sorry, you're a what?" My mom stares at me with such genuine confusion I cannot tell if she is this shocked or truly didn't hear the words that just came out of my mouth.

"I'm an alcoholic," I stammer.

"I don't understand."

Of course, you don't, I thought angrily. The truth is, I was not sure if I was an *alcoholic*, either, but I did know three things.

1. **Alcohol was making my life worse.** Did I drink every day? No. Did something terrible, or embarrassing, happen every time I drank? Also no. But every time something disastrous happened, I was drinking. And that scared the hell out of me. My drinking felt like Russian Roulette. Sure, most times I drank, things were fine. But when I did drink too much and lost control, I often became self-destructive. I got into huge fights with friends and said terrible things I didn't mean . . . often disappearing from the bar without a trace. I drove drunk more times then I would like to admit and slept with strangers regardless of the promises I made to myself in the daylight.

2. **Moderating wasn't working.** I tried all the things, including, but not limited to, not pregaming, not drinking hard liquor, only drinking hard liquor, not taking shots, only drinking shots (*I cannot believe I thought that one was a good idea*), only

drinking wine, only drinking beer (*which I hated the taste of*), measuring my drinks, only drinking on the weekend, not drinking more than three drinks, not drinking alone, and not drinking on an empty stomach. It wasn't even that some of these things didn't work. Sometimes I was able to stick to them for a period of time. But the rules didn't prevent me from putting myself in dangerous situations or making poor choices. I spent an exorbitant amount of time trying to crack the code. I was like a mad scientist. I needed enough alcohol to drown out my social anxiety and make me extroverted, but not so much that I would be unable to hold a conversation or do something embarrassing. I needed enough alcohol to feel confident talking to guys, but not so much that I would sleep with them on the first date. It was absolutely *exhausting*.

3. **I would not be able to become a therapist if I continued drinking this way.** Because my drinking didn't land me in rehab or jail, I was able to continue drinking while I was in graduate school to become a therapist. I showed up to my internship (which was at a drug and alcohol rehab) hungover more times than I would care to admit. I have vague and cringeworthy memories of declaring at my five-year high school reunion (in between deep chugs of cheap red wine, the kind that stains your teeth) that I *loved* helping addicts and alcoholics as if I were different from or better than them. Mind you, that evening I went on to get kicked out of the bar after stealing a bottle of vodka, followed by hooking up with a guy in a stairwell, falling asleep in the hallway of the hotel, and losing the most sentimental piece of jewelry I owned. The denial was thick to say the least.

It was not until a few months later, after a particularly hard night of partying that resulted in me binging and purging (relapsing in my eating disorder), that I woke up covered in my own puke and had to go teach a yoga class at 6 a.m. (while I was completely drunk) that some of the fog started to clear. *What would my clients think if they saw me right now?* I thought. It's one thing to drink and work at an addiction facility, it's another to be getting bombed and showing up to work hungover. *I'm a fraud*, I thought. Hot tears stung my eyes. That was the last day that I drank.

I want to be clear—that day wasn't particularly special. I had moments like it before. I say this because I think there is an unfortunate narrative that tells people they need to "hit rock bottom" because they are only capable of changing on their lowest day. The truth is, I had showed up to work or called out due to being hungover before. I also had recognized the connection between my drinking and eating disorder, and talked about it at length with my therapist. It wasn't my worst drunk or rock bottom by any means. It was just another bad night. The only difference was that on this day when my inner voice said I couldn't go on like this, I listened. And more importantly, I took action. One step. That is all it takes.

So, back to the interaction with my mom . . . I was not sure if I fit the label of an *alcoholic* per say, but I did know I needed a change. I could see the direction that this was heading in and it wasn't pretty. I was fortunate enough to be in group therapy at this time with a few individuals who were getting into recovery. Most of them were going to twelve-step meetings at the time and were able to find a sense of community and connection with others. I went to my first Alcoholics Anonymous (AA) meeting shortly after the last night I drank. There was a part of me that felt like I didn't *deserve* to be there because my drinking wasn't bad enough. I thought, *I'm taking someone's seat who really needs to be here!* When I shared this with others, people were quick to tell me it was denial. I wasn't sure if this was true, but I kept going to meetings. I found a meeting that was a general meeting for anyone in recovery and was geared toward younger people. This group became my support system, my lifeline, and my social life. To this day, some of my best friends are from that meeting.

About This Book

But this isn't a story about *my* drinking, it is a story about *your* drinking. It's a guide that lays out why you drink, how to stop drinking, and how to build a life that you don't need to escape from. It's a book about choice.* Most of us are never truly given the opportunity to question our relationship with alcohol. We are born into a set of cultural ideals that says that alcohol is a healthy part of adult life. We learn that alcohol is fun. It's the glue that holds our social lives together (it gives us something to talk about, it makes us relatable, and signals to other people that we're cool and don't take ourselves too seriously). We learn that alcohol is the preferred way that adults deal with stress. And if, for some reason, you question your relationship with alcohol, you are either a loser or an alcoholic . . . take your pick.

This book isn't a sobriety manifesto, a quitting memoir, or an addiction self-help book. I am not interested in trying to convince you why you should not drink. However, I am of the belief that many of us

---

* The word "choice" can be a controversial one in addiction circles as people who identify as alcoholics or addicts often discuss how they have no choice when it comes to using substances. I want to be clear that when I use the word "choice," I am by no means trying to imply that alcoholics can choose to stop drinking whenever they want, and it is their fault if they don't quit. This book is intended for individuals who are questioning their drinking, want to cut back, or don't identify as alcoholics. I am by no meanings trying to encourage someone who identifies as an alcoholic to stop using that word or quit their twelve-step program.

do not receive proper education about alcohol, and the costs and benefits of it. I don't believe we are informed consumers. We grow up seeing everyone around us drink, we see adults and celebrities and people we look up to drink, and we want to be just like them. We then see it glamorized in TV, movies, social media, and ads. We are sold the idea that the loneliness, disconnection, and pain we feel isn't because we are human (and that life sucks sometimes), it is because we are without a drink in our hand. This book is the guide I wish I had when I was questioning my drinking.

Throughout my years as a therapist, I've learned that almost all of us struggle with addictive patterns in some capacity. However, some patterns of behavior are more socially acceptable (or in some cases downright praised) than others. If you are reading this book, my guess is your addictive pattern is alcohol.

Other common ones include

- Drug use
- Dieting
- Disordered eating (purging, starving, binging, excessive exercise, or a fixation with clean or healthy eating)
- Gambling
- Shopping
- Workaholism/hustle culture
- Romantic relationships or sex

Maybe you have some of these too. The truth is, our addictive behaviors make up only a small portion of what we are actually *dealing* with. A helpful way to understand this phenomenon is through the metaphor of an iceberg. Just like an iceberg, our visible behaviors only make up a small portion of what is going on. The other 85 percent of the iceberg is made up of the patterns, behaviors, and beliefs that create the structure of the iceberg itself. Until you work to heal the deeper part of the iceberg, you will always experience some kind of unhealthy behavior, just like an iceberg cannot exist without some piece of it residing under the surface. This book will focus on alcohol, but it will address other unhealthy patterns (especially disordered eating since that is so common in women) so that you can prevent addiction switching, or the whack-a-mole phenomenon when you get one thing under control only to have another pattern pop up in its place.

While this book will give you practical tools and tips for how to stop or reduce your alcohol intake, the majority of the book will help you address deeper reasons for your addictive patterns . . . or the submerged part of the iceberg. In the first section, **why you drink**, you will learn more about your mind and how shame and trauma are intertwined with your drinking. In the second part I discuss tools for **how to stop drinking**. This includes reparenting, emotion regulation, boundaries, and all the essential skills you will need to be able to heal the root of why you are drinking in the first place. In the final section, **make it stick**, we will talk about common pitfalls of early sobriety, how to socialize, date, have sex, and deal with your family and current relationships without alcohol.

I also discuss moderation tips for mindful drinking so you can decide if you want to quit completely or experiment with sober curiosity and moderation. I am of the belief that anyone, for any reason, can explore their relationship with alcohol. As my friend Millie Gooch says, "You do not have to wait until a fire engulfs your house in flames before you try and put it out. If you see a small blaze starting in the form of problem drinking, it's okay to put it out before it burns down your house."[1] If you picked up this book, my guess is you are noticing the fires of unhealthy drinking. Think of this book as a fire extinguisher; use it to quell the flames and put the whole fire out if you choose.

This book is not just written by someone who quit drinking, it is also written by a licensed therapist who specializes in helping people change their relationship with alcohol. This means the information and story I tell are not just mine but snapshots of three women who together sum up the most common thoughts, fears, concerns, pitfalls, and struggles that I see in my clinical work and in research on this subject. Throughout the book we will follow these women and their journeys in exploring sobriety.

- **Andrea**, a twenty-four-year-old Peruvian woman who immigrated to the United States as a child. She is now in medical school, engaged, and discovering how dependent she is on alcohol in order to feel social and let off steam on her days off.
- **Tara**, a twenty-one-year-old white woman who has been in and out of rehab for the past few years. She knows for sure she needs to stop drinking but has a nasty habit of self-sabotage. Throughout her sobriety she uncovers the truth about her sexuality.
- **Brianna**, a thirty-four-year-old Black woman who is married with two children. She finds herself relying on alcohol to deal with the transition to motherhood and quell the feelings of guilt about being a working mother.

These women are characters amalgamated from nearly fifty cases, so that I could be sure almost everyone who reads this book can find themselves in some aspect of each of these characters. While I firmly believe anyone, regardless of gender, can enjoy and learn from this book, this book does focus on the female experience of sobriety and the unique things women, especially millennial women, have to navigate within alcohol culture, such as mommy wine culture, eating disorders, and perfectionism.

By the end of reading this book, you will fully understand how and why you drink (or do any other addictive behavior) and create a life that you don't need to escape from. Once you finish this book, you will understand how connected your relationship with alcohol is to your relationship with other areas of your life. This will give you the opportunity to make an informed decision about your drinking. In the therapy world, we call this informed consent. If a therapist doesn't go over with a client how therapy works, the costs, and a therapist's policies, education, and rates verbally, therapy is unethical. Think of this book as your informed consent about drinking. Whether you choose to go back to drinking or not at the end of this book is your decision. My job is not to convince you. My job is to give you the knowledge to create a life you love, one that is not perfect but is messy and real and one you are fully present for. A life without alcohol is possible and, dare I say, magical? Whether you choose that is up to you.

Part 1

Why You Drink

Reevaluating Your Relationship with Alcohol

Chapter 1

Would Your Life Be Better Without Alcohol?

I'd say the most common thing to do in the year before quitting booze is to hunch over a laptop and miserably type Am I an alcoholic? into Google at 1am.
—Catherine Gray

"It's not like I can't go a day without drinking," Andrea says earnestly. She looks put together as always, wearing a button-down shirt tucked neatly into a high waisted skirt. A self-described perfectionist, Andrea and I have been working together for two months. In the past few sessions, we have been talking more about her drinking habits and how it impacts her anxiety, her relationship with her new fiancé, and her low self-worth, which she says she has struggled with since she immigrated to America from Peru at age nine.

"I understand," I say, and I do, more than she knows. I myself sat on a similar looking couch and said the same exact thing to my therapist almost a decade ago.

"Sometimes I can go months without drinking. It isn't even that difficult," Andrea says, matter-of-factly. Her face searches mine for validation. I can tell she wants me to agree with her and move on to another topic, but she also knows me well enough to know I'm not going to let that happen.

"I believe you," I say. And I do. She smiles.

Here's the thing—I'm sure Andrea doesn't drink every day and she probably has had periods of time when she didn't drink. It's just that the frequency of her drinking isn't her issue. The issue is the impact that drinking has on her life. The truth is that Andrea, like many other women who come through my door, do not come to see me for "alcohol addiction" or their inability to stop drinking. They end up on my couch because they are depressed, anxious, have eating disorders, low self-esteem, don't get along with their families, keep dating the wrong people, want more meaningful friendships, are unfulfilled with their careers, or any number of other things that seem to have nothing to do with alcohol consumption or any other addictive pattern of behavior . . . except they actually do. Of course, this is not to say that every one of these issues is caused by alcohol consumption or that every one of my clients needs to stop drinking to work through their issues. Quite the contrary. However, the way we, as a society, discuss alcohol consumption and alcohol use disorder is unhelpful at best and harmful at worst. In order to fully understand this, I think it's important to dive into the history of alcoholism so we can understand how the stigma evolved and is perpetuated and how our current models of treating it are unsatisfactory in dealing with the current reality of the drinking landscape.

Despite the fact that recent studies show that individuals in the United States are drinking more in the past few years than ever before, and women especially are experiencing increasing health complications due to alcohol consumption, it is more stigmatizing to not consume alcohol than to consume it. Most women are more afraid of consuming sugar and artificially flavored foods than alcohol. Never mind the fact that alcohol, also known as ethanol, is the same substance we use to fuel cars. (Seriously, look it up if you don't believe me.)

Alcohol is tightly woven into the fabric of our lives. Every major holiday in the United States incorporates alcohol. We use it to bond, connect, and commemorate weddings, funerals, dates, social events, good news, bad news, and almost everything in between. If someone says they don't drink, we often assume the person is either religious, pregnant, or an alcoholic. In our society, those are the only reasonable reasons to abstain. Most doctors still tout the heart-healthy benefits of a glass of red wine without inquiring into the patient's relationship with alcohol or how it may be causing or exacerbating their problems.

Andrea stares out the window and a childlike smile appears on her face as she sees a squirrel hopping across the window ledge. She appears to forget where she is for a moment. She then quickly turns back to me and re-furrows her eyebrows seriously.

"It's just—I'm not an alcoholic. I know I'm not. I looked it up." I take a deep breath as Andrea unfolds a piece of paper that she tells me she printed out from a website. Of course, Andrea printed out the criteria for alcohol use disorder. Our work is just beginning.

So often the question that clinicians (or in this case, concerned individuals searching the internet) focus on answering is "Is this person an alcoholic?"

Here's the backstory—the term "alcoholism" was coined by a Swedish physician in 1849 and it became largely adopted throughout the world. This term referred mostly to the physiological damage of long-term drinking, not to any of the mental impacts of the disease. In 1918, when the American Medico-Psychological Association (which later became the American Psychiatric Association) created the first handbook of mental disorders, alcoholism was characterized by symptoms like hallucinations, tremors, delirium, amnesia, and paranoia. Safe to say, you had to have a pretty severe case to be diagnosed with alcoholism at this time. However, it is unclear what an acceptable level of alcohol ingestion looked like at the time considering this manual's publication coincided with the temperance movement and prohibition.

Soon after the end of prohibition, in 1935, Alcoholics Anonymous (AA) was formed. The organization believed alcoholics had a physical allergy to alcohol which prevented them from drinking like normal people. And while they could never safely consume any amount of alcohol, they could recover and become functioning members of society if they admitted their powerlessness over alcohol, confessed their mistakes, and made amends for their wrongs. This was a huge breakthrough because up until then, alcoholics were widely considered to be morally bankrupt and disgraceful members of society with no hope of changing or recovering. For the first time, alcoholics had a safe place to get support and help rather than be sent away to rot in an asylum. (However, it's important to note that AA originated as a puritanical religious group, which makes a lot of the program steeped in morality. The program's rigidity can breed shame as people are taught that there are right and wrong ways to act, think, and recover. While AA was a revolution at the time and still continues to help millions of people, the program has been largely unchanged since its creation, which originally did not allow women or people of color to participate.[1])

The stigma against alcoholics persisted throughout the twentieth century. It wasn't until the third edition of the *Diagnostic Statistical Manual of Mental Disorders* (DSM) was published in 1980 that alcoholism was classified as a primary disorder (rather than a personality disorder, which contributed to the stigma). Psychiatrists expanded the definition to include individuals who may not have developed a physical dependence or physiological damage. Of course, this led to a continuous debate among experts about how to separate "problem drinkers" from "alcoholics." Fast forward to the current edition, DSM-5, released in 2013, which effectively created a spectrum of Alcohol Use Disorder (AUD) with three subtypes: mild, moderate, and severe.

Replacing the word "abuse," which conjures negative connotations of destruction and harm, with "use" has made a difference in destigmatizing the disorder. Additionally, making it a spectrum allows healthcare providers to focus less on trying to decipher which disorder an individual has and instead recognize a range of symptoms that point to an individual having an issue with alcohol consumption. Adding in the "mild" subtype also makes it easier for individuals who don't meet the criteria for alcohol disorder to get professional help. Unfortunately, a lot of stigma remains. I see it all the time in my practice. Due to AA's popularity, most people still believe that they must label themselves as an "alcoholic" if they want to stop drinking. And given this fraught history with the label, it's no surprise why the average individual resists calling herself an alcoholic.

I don't blame Andrea for trying to convince me. The impulse makes perfect sense considering the enduring stigma. If you ask someone what they think an alcoholic looks like, most say an old man, who lost his family, home, and job, sitting on a stoop swigging from a bottle wrapped in a brown paper bag. Of course, Andrea, the twenty-four-year-old engaged, marathon-running med student does not see herself as an alcoholic.

"Andrea, let me ask," I say, "what exactly makes someone an 'alcoholic'?"

She thinks for a moment. "Well, I typically think of someone who drinks every day, or can't stop drinking. The image I have in my head is typically an older man with drinking problems, like *mi bisabuelo*. He was probably an alcoholic. Or there were definitely girls I went to high school with who were getting in tons of trouble for underage drinking and then later DUIs. It wouldn't surprise me if one of them was an alcoholic."

"Ah, so someone either is an alcoholic or they're not. They can't become one?" I ask, trying to understand her point of view.

"I mean, I'm in medical school. I've studied alcoholism. It's a disease and I know genetics play a large role. So according to the bio-psycho-social disease model, people are probably born with it, but then the problems aren't revealed until later. Nobody in my immediate family is an alcoholic, so I don't see how that could be me."

Despite the APA's attempts to destigmatize alcoholism by creating a spectrum and renaming it "alcohol use disorder," the term "alcoholism" is still widely used. Part of this is because Alcoholics Anonymous has long been considered the dominant and only effective treatment for alcohol use disorders. Unfortunately, we don't have much language for individuals to use to examine their relationship with alcohol without admitting they are an alcoholic.

This means that if someone thinks they may have a problem with alcohol, they google "Am I an alcoholic?" They check out some lists and typically find comfort in discovering that they don't meet all the criteria. There are lots of tests online; Andrea has found the official eleven-point criteria from the current DSM for diagnosing alcohol use disorder. Keep in mind, the DSM is not intended for self-diagnosis. However, websites often list the criteria and say you can easily diagnose yourself, which of course leads to situations like the current one I am in with Andrea.

"Can I read it to you?" Andrea asks. I know the criteria by heart, but something tells me it's important for Andrea to go through with her presentation so she can feel fully heard. "Go ahead," I say. Andrea flattens her piece of paper and clears her throat.

1. Drinking more, or for a longer period of time than you intended.

Andrea says, "Yes, I've done that this year, but this just seems like a pretty ridiculous criterion. But yes, I'll count it. That's one."

2. Having a desire to cut down or stop drinking but being unsuccessful.

"No, I haven't been trying to quit and failing at it," Andrea responds.

3. Spending a lot of time obtaining alcohol, drinking or recovering from it.

"No."

4. Having a strong desire to use alcohol.

"No, I think I like it a regular amount," Andrea says flatly.

5. Being unable to fulfill major role responsibilities at work, home or school due to drinking.

"No," she quips.

6. Continuing to drink even though it is causing strain to your relationships."

Andrea thinks for a moment, "No."

I'm surprised at this one, considering our last session was about her relationship with her fiancé and how they have been getting into fights when they are drinking. He had made a particularly biting comment about how she acts like a different person when she is drunk. But it's hard to be completely transparent about your drinking habits if you are afraid you will be diagnosed with a disease and forced to quit.

Andrea and I continue to go through the list and she responds no to all the remaining questions.

7. Giving up or cutting back on important activities because of drinking.

8. Continuing to drink despite being in situations that are physically hazardous.

9. Continuing to drink even though it is causing physical or psychological problems.

10. Having to drink more than you once did in order to get the same effect you want.

11. Experiencing withdrawal symptoms after drinking alcohol.

"So, there you have it," Andrea says proudly, "I only have one out of eleven. Not an alcoholic."

"What if asking yourself *Am I an alcoholic?* is the wrong question?" I suggest. "Instead, my question to you is, would your life be better without alcohol?"

Andrea hesitates and bites her lip. It seems like she wasn't expecting to hear this response from me. "I don't know. I mean on one hand, yes. I think it's safe to say everyone's life would probably be better without alcohol."

"What about you?" I say. "How would your, Andrea's, life be better without alcohol?" She playfully rolls her eyes because we've talked before about how she tends to use generalizations when she is uncomfortable.

"Well, Jack and I would probably get along better, and I would definitely feel better and have more time, but in other ways it would make my life worse. It's important for me to be able to unwind at the end of the week. Med school is making me go insane. Going out to the bar is one of the few ways I bond with my classmates. I think I would actually be more stressed about not drinking than continuing to drink. The idea of having to explain it to people . . ." She shakes her head. "I'm going to be a doctor!"

I sigh. This is what stigma looks like. And this is how it impacts people. Maybe you are one of them.

A New Way

When it comes to the treatment and understanding of mental health disorders, our society has made huge progress in the past century. Mental health issues are less taboo, more people than ever are seeking professional therapy and treatment, and we have progressed to creating spectrums when it comes to diagnoses of mental health issues. However, alcohol use disorder is one that still gets categorized as black and white; you are either a normal drinker who can (and should!)

drink with abandon, or you are an alcoholic and must abstain completely. People assume that anyone who does not drink must have a problem, which in a perverse way leads to the stigmatization of abstinence. As Annie Grace, author of *This Naked Mind*, shrewdly points out, "Alcohol is the only drug on earth you have to justify not taking."[2] Unfortunately, when we focus solely on discovering if the person meets criteria to be diagnosed with a disorder, we drastically limit the larger conversation; one that starts with the question . . . *would my life be better without alcohol?*

According to the National Institute for Alcohol Abuse and Alcoholism, 26.45 percent of American adults admit to heavy drinking in the past year, with only 5.8 percent being diagnosed with Alcohol Use Disorder. With these statistics in mind, it is clear that many people are left out of the conversation. I believe we need to look at alcohol use on a wider spectrum. Many people do not get to honestly assess how alcohol may be impacting their well-being. Instead, I believe we need to create an entirely new term: **Disordered Drinking**.

I came up with this term based on my experience working with individuals with eating disorders. In the current DSM, there are a few different eating disorder diagnoses and, like Alcohol Use Disorder, individuals need to meet certain criteria for diagnosis. However, there is also a concept called "disordered eating," wherein an individual displays some characteristics and symptoms of an eating disorder but doesn't fully meet all criteria. Studies have shown that individuals who engage in disordered eating are much more likely to develop a full-blown eating disorder. However, if someone gets treatment in the early stages, they have a greatly improved chance of getting well. I find time and time again that it's easier to talk to my clients about food and have them honestly look at how dieting or binging is negatively impacting their life than it is for them to discuss alcohol. Women are aware that it's very common to have some unhealthy behaviors around food. We can talk about this without someone assuming that I am going to diagnose them with an eating disorder. I can't say the same when it comes to talking about drinking habits—and this sadly prevents millions of women from honestly assessing their behaviors and changing them for the better.

So rather than stepping on a soapbox and listing all the reasons you may be an alcoholic, I encourage you to honestly assess if your life would be better without alcohol. That's all I'm asking. I imagine you're already thinking that, since you're reading this book! You don't need to hit rock bottom or meet some criteria in order to stop drinking. If you believe your life would be better without alcohol, that is the only reason you need. Here are some things to consider as you evaluate your relationship with alcohol and how it might be impacting your life. Explore these questions honestly and without judgment. The answers are only for you; it's safe for you to be real. There are no right answers. In reflecting on these questions, you will be able to holistically assess whether your life would be better without alcohol. If one of the questions doesn't apply to you or resonate with you, go ahead and skip it.

Exercise: Grab a pen and a piece of paper and answer the following questions.

- What role does alcohol serve in my life? How does it solve problems for me? For example, does it soothe my feelings of awkwardness at social events? Does it help me relax at the end of a long day? Does it make dating and sex easier? Does it help soothe my loneliness?
- What specific situations, events, or activities feel easier with a drink in my hand? Weddings, restaurants, blind dates, flying?

- How is drinking negatively impacting my relationships with my family? Friends? Community?
- What do people in my life say about my drinking habits?
- How does drinking negatively impact my mental health? Does my anxiety increase after a night out of drinking? Does drinking worsen my depression? Do I get flashbacks or have trauma resurface when I drink?
- What is it like to wake up after a night of drinking? What emotions do I feel?
- How often do I do things when I drink that I regret the next day? What is that experience like?
- Do I often make promises to myself that I will "never drink again?" or that I will drink less? How long do those promises last? What does it feel like to break promises to myself?
- Do I drink alone? Why? What is the connection between feeling lonely and consuming alcohol?
- Do I use alcohol to deal with my emotions? How?
- How does alcohol affect my sleep?
- Do I have a history of disordered eating? Do I notice the connection between drinking and eating patterns or self-esteem? Do I ever skip meals in order to accommodate for the calories I am going to be drinking? How would my food and body image improve if I didn't drink?
- How does drinking impact my performance at work?
- Have my goals and values shifted to accommodate my drinking? If so, which ones?
- How interconnected is drinking with my social connections? What role does it play in my friendships? Which friendships would endure without alcohol?

- As a parent, how does drinking impact my ability to parent and be present with my kids?
- How does drinking alcohol interfere with my ability to take care of myself?
- Would my life be better without alcohol? Why or why not?

An Important Note

Although I never want to encourage anyone to continue to drink alcohol if they are motivated to stop, as a therapist who believes in harm reduction and safety, I understand that quitting doesn't look the same for everyone. If you live in an environment that is unsafe (for example, you live with an abuser or you feel unsafe all the time because your emotional health is so dysregulated you constantly have flashbacks), or you don't have access to having your basic needs (food, water, shelter, safety, clothes, sleep) met, I do not recommend quitting drinking cold turkey. If drinking is the only thing keeping you going and you have no other coping skills and don't have the ability to create safety for yourself, I recommend cutting back on drinking slowly as you integrate skills and tools from this book. I believe in harm reduction first. Too many individuals have been shamed on this journey by not being able to become abstinent. In these situations, I recommend finding a licensed therapist (see resources at the back of this book) and focusing on creating safety and basic well-being before changing your drinking habits.

Chapter 2

Evolutionary Psychology: It's in Your Brain

You can take the person out of the Stone Age,
but you can't take the Stone Age out of the person.
—Nigel Nicholson

"What if there's nothing wrong with you?"

"I don't understand," Tara, a twenty-one-year-old white woman, groans and rolls her eyes. They are icy blue, heavily coated with eyeliner, and pop against her freshly dyed pink hair.

"Maybe your brain is acting the way it was wired to."

"Amanda, have you forgotten who you are talking to? I am all kinds of messed up. I have been to rehab three times and had my stomach pumped twice. I'm an alcoholic. There is absolutely something wrong with me."

"I understand why you think that way," I say carefully. With all the therapists Tara has seen, she is jaded to say the least, and I don't want her to shut down as I challenge her self-deprecating thinking. "But do you know much about your brain? From an evolutionary perspective?"

"Well, no matter what I do or try it doesn't seem like I'm ever happy. And my parents say that I've always been like that since I've been a kid, so I feel like I will just never be happy no matter what. So, I may as well drink."

"Because that makes you happy?" I ask, statistically.

"No," Tara says rolling her eyes. "Because drinking at least makes the pain of being alive more tolerable."

"So, when you think about it, your brain is actually really smart."

"What do you mean?"

"Well, you know that being alive is painful, and one of the ways you have adapted to the pain of being alive is by numbing yourself, in this case with alcohol. So, your brain is actually adapting, trying to keep you alive. The truth is, Tara, from an evolutionary perspective, your brain doesn't actually care if you are happy or not. Your brain cares about keeping you alive. Even if that means you are miserable."

"Huh," Tara said as she slid down in the plush velvet couch in my office. "Never thought of it like that before."

Here's the deal. Our society teaches us that being happy all the time is "normal" and that should be our baseline. We live in a culture that is obsessed with happiness. Almost every client who takes a seat on my blue velvet couch ends up saying at some point or another, "Why can't I just be happy?" . . . as if the opposite of suffering is happiness. Modern spiritual and self-help leaders especially love to talk about this when they promote their teachings, as a way to inspire individuals to "reclaim their natural state," often referencing giggly children as evidence that "your natural state is joy!"* And if you recite enough affirmations, drink enough celery juice, and set enough boundaries, you

---

* This quote is attributed to Wayne Dwyer.

will be able to avoid all negative emotions. It's a huge reason why we drink, diet, shop, gamble, or become perfectionists . . . because advertising and the media tell us that if we drink this beverage, look like this celebrity, or have their lifestyle, we will finally be happy! Evolution, however, tells us a different story.

Our brains and bodies evolved to do a few things: eat, breathe, drink water, sleep, go to the bathroom, and procreate. All other things we do, such as running, jumping, hiding, hunting, building shelters, and forming social bonds evolved in order to better meet those basic needs. However, the most important job our brain had was to keep us alive. As Russ Harris says, "The primitive mind was basically a 'Don't get killed' device."[1] In many ways, our "natural state" isn't happiness, it's survival. And while emotionally suffering can negatively impact your health, and there is no value in misery, being joyful or happy is also not always evolutionarily advantageous. You aren't more likely to have kids if you're happy. You aren't even more likely to be successful or powerful or have more resources if you're happy. In fact, sometimes our anxiety and fear can actually drive us to get things done. Want to know what was evolutionarily advantageous? Being careful.

Over the millions of years of evolution, the people that were careful and likely to hesitate when they saw something in the bushes were the ones more likely to survive. The more careful our ancestors were while also being driven to never be satisfied (more food, more shelter, more children), the more successful they and their genes were. Thus, we come from a long lineage of ancestors who were careful and took calculated risks. Our ancestors, like all wild species, constantly surveyed their surroundings to make sure they were safe while also trying to get as many resources as possible. As the saying goes, eat or be eaten.

Our hunter-gatherer ancestors, like all other primates, were highly social animals and lived in small groups of people. Without strong jaws, sharp teeth, or lightning-fast legs, humans' survival depended on living and cooperating together. Because of this, it was extremely important that everyone in your clan trusted you and generally liked you, or you were at risk of being kicked to the curb. And the curb, in this case, meant almost certain death. Therefore, natural selection also shaped us to be highly invested in what other people thought about us. However, we were evolved to only care about the opinions of people who knew us intimately, and that was a maximum of 150 people.[2] We were not evolved to be in touch with the thoughts and opinions of literally billions of people on the planet, most of whom do not know us but have the ability to send a hateful comment based on five words we wrote on the internet. It's no wonder that social media usage is linked with high rates of depression and anxiety.

Furthermore, the "threats" we now experience in our modern society are typically not life threatening. We no longer are in danger of being eaten by a lion, we are in danger of being called out at work, failing an assignment at school, or being embarrassed by our kids' meltdown at the playground. Now, being careful and caring so much about what others think backfires on us. Our modern-day version of "survival" often looks like trying to fit in with your friends, not speaking up at work when you disagree with a company policy, or laughing at your father-in-law's joke. For most of us, we spend our lives trying to make it through another day without ruffling too many feathers but also trying to be successful and well liked.

In the past fifty years, with the rise of consumerism, individualism, and the nuclear family, in addition to a high divorce rate and decrease in birth rate, more people than ever are experiencing loneliness. We live in a complete paradox, where we are simultaneously more connected than ever through the internet and social media (to people who don't know, love, or care about us) while also being more isolated than ever. We can interact with thousands of people a day from behind a screen while never experiencing a hug from a loved one or a conversation in person. Research findings indicate that individuals who struggle with loneliness are more likely to use alcohol to alleviate their symptoms,[3] a phenomenon that was further proven by studies during the COVID-19 pandemic.[4] Scientists have already been sounding the alarm that the United States is experiencing a loneliness epidemic, and it appears that the pandemic has only made that worse.[5] Our brains evolved to live in a hunter-gatherer society, not in the modern society we live in today, which is why we tend to suffer so much.

The Trap of Innovation

It's easy to forget, but for millions of years, even after we discovered how to create fire, humans were squarely in the middle of the food chain (often eating leftovers, foraging, or hunting small game). It was not until around seventy thousand years ago that a genetic mutation occurred, which transformed the way we thought, learned, and communicated with one another.[6] Historians dub this the Cognitive Revolution as it allowed for large-scale human cooperation. This may have catapulted us to the top of the food chain, but it was not until twelve thousand years ago, with the Agricultural Revolution, that we began to settle on land and farm. Humans went from spending most of our time traveling from place to place, foraging, hunting, and eating a wide variety of foods to eventually subsisting on a few foods that were able to be grown, like wheat, rice, and corn. The transformation from hunter-gatherers to farmers was a slow one over time, with human beings not seeing the irreversible consequences of the decision until it was too late to go back. Historians argue that while farming was innovative and seemed like a phenomenal idea, this change was actually a trap, as nomads had a significantly higher quality of life than farmers who became dependent on their land.

Our modern-day life is also filled with many of these traps as well. The unfortunate truth is that when any new invention is created, it has unintended consequences that we cannot foresee until we are experiencing them. With innovation, we become dependent on new technology and then cannot return to how things were before, even if our quality of life was potentially better before the change. Maybe you have experienced this one. Once you adapt to having the newest iPhone, it's hard to go back to an old version. It is also why our happiness or joy after getting something new tends to wear off and return to baseline. This phenomenon is known as the hedonic treadmill and it is a huge driver for humans to constantly seek more and be chronically unsatisfied. Additionally, the problems we fix with new innovation often create problems that are even more complex to solve. Take for example the invention of the telephone. It was an amazing invention that saved tons of time. Before it, our primary way to communicate with others was through mail and telegrams. But then in-house phones weren't good enough, so we invented cell phones to be able to communicate with people at all times. Now our cell phones are tiny computers, and we are so dependent on them that people get into car accidents because they cannot stop using them while driving, which is a much more complicated problem to solve.

Indeed, one could argue that most of humanity's struggles, including those in regard to addiction and mental health, are "the result of the way our hunter-gatherer minds interact with our current post-industrial environment, with its mega-cities, airplanes, telephones and computers. This environment gives us more material resources and longer lives than those enjoyed by any previous generation, but it often makes us feel alienated, depressed and pressured."[7] Our brains did not adapt to live in the world that we currently live in. While this information alone does not change our brains, it can massively cut down on the amount of judgment and shame we feel. This in itself makes a huge difference in our healing. Almost every time I meet with a client, the first obstacle we have to work through is not what is actually going on in their life or their current emotional state but their judgment, shame, and emotional reaction to what is going on. If you are reading this book, my guess is you have experienced what I am talking about. You judge yourself for your drinking habits but aren't sure if you should stop or can stop. Hang tight, we'll dive into this more in Chapter 4.

The Invention of Stress

During the Stone Age, people were primarily concerned with getting enough food, not pissing off the people that they lived with, and staying alive. Therefore, even after the Cognitive Revolution, when people developed the capacity to, say, worry about things that have not happened yet, there was not a tremendous amount to worry about. Stressors existed, but stress was not really a concept because it was short-lived. Hiding from a mountain lion was stressful, but it did not last more than a few hours. The lion either found and killed you, or you escaped, and the mountain lion found something else to eat for dinner. If you escaped, you rejoined your community and rested as your body healed and returned to normal, a process called allostasis (the process your body undergoes after a stressor or stimuli knocks you out of homeostasis).

Our bodies and brains evolved to be in short periods of life-or-death scenarios, aka what we call the fight-flight-freeze response. During this process, your body undergoes many physiological changes as your bloodstream floods with hormones, which increase your chance for survival. To name a few, your heart rate and breathing increase to pump more oxygen to your muscles; your vision and hearing sharpens; your pain tolerance increases; your body stops doing anything that is not essential to survival, such as digestion, in order to save energy. It needs to make sure you live long enough to use the food you just ate. The experience of freezing happens as a last resort, when your body recognizes that the best-case scenario for you to survive is essentially to "play dead" until the threat goes away. As Emily Nagoski says, "In the middle of the gas-pedal of stress response, your brain slams on the brakes—the parasympathetic nervous system swamping the sympathetic—and you shut down."[8] In nature, a mammal's response after successfully surviving using freeze is to shake and move as it releases the energy and hormones that flooded its system. This is how your body recalibrates itself and learns that it is safe so that all processes can go back to normal. Some other common symptoms of "discharging stress activation"[9] as Elizabeth Stanley calls it, include crying, yawning, sweating, itching, coughing, or stomach gurgling.

In our current society, though most of us do not often find ourselves in life-or-death situations, our bodies still react as though we are in physical danger. As we sit in traffic, our bloodstreams flood with adrenaline, and yet there is nowhere to run and release that energy. As we worry about our child's illness, our heart races and we want to fight, but there is nothing we can do, and the stress is not leaving anytime soon. As a result, our body never gets the memo that we are safe, the danger has passed, and we can recalibrate. We do not complete the stress cycle,[10] and many of us live in a constant state of sustained stress. This can create many physical and psychological problems for us. Living in a constant state of high blood pressure, for example, wears down

Fight - Flight - Freeze Response

Heart Rate	Increases to pump more blood and increase oxygen to your muscles
Lungs	Breathing quickens to increase oxygen
Blood	Blood thickens as your body prepares for potential injuries
Skin	Increases sweating; flushed skin
Eyes	Pupils dilate, increases peripheral vision so you can see better
Ears	Hearing abilities increase

your heart and blood vessels. This is a classic evolutionary example of how our bodies' phenomenal adaptations at keeping us alive now can create a host of diseases, as our response to stress causes us more damage that the stressor itself. Furthermore, our minds allow us to also replay stressful events and predict potential new stressful events that may happen. And our body can react with the same intensity whether this scenario is real or imaginary.

As Robert Sapolsky says, "Unlike less cognitively sophisticated species, we can turn on the stress-response by thinking about the potential stressors that may throw us out of homeostatic balance in the future."[11] Most of us do not learn this concept or learn how to appropriately deal with stress, and drinking is one of the most common ways individuals in modern times deal with stress after a long day. But drinking a glass of wine at the end of the night does not bring your body back into homeostasis. It does the opposite and forces your body to release more chemicals to metabolize and rid itself of the foreign substance, leaving us even more depleted and unbalanced than before we drank.

"Well, Tara, what do you think?" I say.

"I think that's good to know. It makes sense. I still think I'm messed up though."

"I know," I say playfully, "I didn't think it would be that easy to convince you."

"It doesn't change the fact that I've been to rehab three times and I'll probably have to go back again, and I don't have a job, and I'm essentially not a fully functioning adult."

"It doesn't," I say. "Knowledge about why we are the way we are does not change the past. But it does create awareness, which is often the first step in change. If we aren't aware of our behavior or why we are doing something, it is harder to change it."

"All right, what's my homework assignment this week?" Tara asks as she starts rummaging through her purse for her sunglasses. She always keeps a firm eye on the clock, ensuring she is ready to go at the exact minute her session ends, as if she can't stand to be in therapy a minute longer. I thankfully know this has more to do with her dis-comfort with therapy than with me.

"I want you to notice how much you catch yourself beating yourself up and try to remember what we talked about. Try to remember how your brain evolved and that there is nothing wrong with you."

"Okay, see you next week," Tara says, as she closes my door.

Chapter 3

The Impacts of Trauma

Trauma is not what happens to you. Trauma is what happens inside of you as a result of what happened to you.

—Dr. Gabor Maté

"I just don't understand why I can't get it to stick," Brianna, a thirty-four-year-old Black woman says, as she fidgets with her bracelet. "I mean I can stop drinking for months at a time. Yet here I am, still sitting on your couch . . . still talking about the same damn thing."

"Well, your problem isn't being able to stop drinking, Brianna," I say, "it's staying stopped."

"Ugh, I don't really know if I even need to stop drinking. Or maybe I don't want to. I don't know . . ." Brianna's gaze drifts off. I can see her wheels spinning. "I just feel like if I *really* had a problem, I wouldn't be able to stop so easily. Maybe I just like drinking. Maybe I am making this more complicated than it is. . . ."

This train of thought is not that uncommon. Because we have an idea as a culture of what an "alcoholic" is (someone who is unable to stop drinking), the ability to easily stop can make individuals think that their drinking isn't an issue.

"What if my problem is trying to stop? What if that is making me want to drink more? If I stopped trying to stop drinking, I wouldn't be struggling with this."

I smile. A typical therapist's response to this statement would be to talk about how the client is in denial and how denial is a quintessential characteristic of alcoholism, which proves they are an alcoholic. But I'm not that type of therapist. "That may be true, but . . . "

Brianna jumps in. "You think I'm nuts, don't you?"

"I don't think you're nuts," I say with a smile.

"You think I'm an alcoholic, huh?"

"You know how I feel about that word," I say. "I understand what you mean, I really do. And you are right, if you never tried to stop drinking again, you would not be struggling with trying to stay sober. However, I think we need to remember why you initially wanted to stop drinking."

Brianna started seeing me after she had stopped drinking for a month. She has successfully stopped drinking for long periods of time. Most recently, she stopped drinking for two and half years when she got pregnant with her elder child, Mia, and then was sober for the first year of her life and through her pregnancy with her younger, Eric. Eric is now four years old, and Brianna has been in and out of sobriety, often stopping for a few months before starting to drink again.

"I get absolutely terrible hangovers. I feel like I'm not able to be present with my kids because I'm looking forward to that glass of wine at the end of the day. It makes my anxiety worse. I just like who I am better when I'm not drinking." Hope spreads across Brianna's face as she says this.

"Those seem like great reasons to me," I say.

"Then why is it so hard for me to stop? I don't even drink that much when I'm drinking. I just drink two or three glasses of wine a night. A lot of my friends drink more than me. Nobody thinks I have a problem."

"The only person that gets to say if it is a problem is you, Brianna. And you're right, I don't even think it's necessarily 'a problem.' Your life isn't falling apart, your job isn't at risk, many things that lead people to stop drinking are not an issue for you. But this is *your* life, and only you get to decide what works for you and what doesn't. And it's clear that your life is much better when you aren't drinking."

"Yeah, but I can't seem to make that happen. It just shouldn't be so hard. I don't get it." Brianna slumps over and sighs.

We have reached the point in therapy I like to call the "come to Jesus moment." It's the point where scratching the surface is not cutting it anymore. Maybe the issue is more complex than we realized, and we need to reevaluate, or maybe it's finally time to address the deeper issues a client has been putting off chatting about for months. In order to do this, I have to address what is happening in the room currently, and our relationship (the one between the client and myself). Addressing what is happening for someone is one of the most vulnerable things we can talk about. As a result, the conversation typically goes one of three ways. One, the client declines the invitation to go deeper in some capacity and it becomes clear we will end therapy. Two, the client is honest about what is going on, but then leaves the session and is horrified by her authenticity and then cancels sessions moving forward. Three, the client accepts the invitation, and we are able to cultivate a deeper and more authentic relationship that transforms the therapy process. Of course, sometimes it can be a combination. I really enjoy working with Brianna; I hope she will be number three.

"I think it may be helpful to look at some of the deeper reasons you may drink," I say. "I know we've talked about the social pressure that comes with your friends and of course the stress of being a mom, but I wonder if you've ever thought about how your upbringing and earlier events in life may have impacted you."

"So, you mean my childhood?" she asks, and I nod. I can tell this statement makes Brianna uncomfortable. Brianna has avoided the conversation of talking about her childhood or her past in general and probably for good reason. As a therapist, my job is made up of calculated risks. Will probing this client on this issue create a breakthrough or a breakdown? Will challenging them strengthen our relationship or push it over the edge? For the most successful therapists, it's a gentle dynamic of push and pull. Similar to the process of lifting weights, we create mini tears in our relationship in order to strengthen it later.

"Growing up, things were definitely tough at times. My dad died of lung cancer when I was twelve, and my mom had to work two jobs in order to keep us afloat. It felt like I lost both my parents that year, so thank god for my grandparents. They essentially raised us." Brianna stares off, appearing to be deep in a memory.

"That sounds incredibly difficult," I say.

"Yeah, but what are you gonna do? You live and you keep going, because you have to." I notice that Brianna switches from identifying personally with what she is saying, to using the word "you," which is often a way we detach and depersonalize our pain.

"Well, I do think this is important to explore. I think some of your earlier experiences may be connected with your drinking. Even if you don't think about your dad's death, for example, when you are drinking, it's helpful to understand how your brain learned to cope with the loss when you were younger because this impacts how you cope today."

"Okay . . . that makes sense," Brianna says. "But I don't think I have trauma or anything. I've never been raped; my parents never laid a hand on me. There was no abuse. As a Black person, people always assume that there was abuse. Growing up, after my dad died, teachers and stuff always assumed he was in prison or was shot. They assumed he was probably a drug dealer. My dad was the most straitlaced person."

"That must have been so hard to deal with, especially being so young and already dealing with this on top of the grief of losing your dad," I say.

Brianna starts to tear up. "Yeah, it really sucked."

"We definitely do not have to use the word 'trauma' if you don't like it, and I want you to know that trauma is not just sexual, physical, or emotional abuse. Trauma is many things. Trauma is anything that is a deeply distressing experience, that overwhelms us, makes us feel powerless, and shakes our sense of self. It's often described when an experience is too much, too soon, or too fast for our bodies to process."

"So, losing my dad could be considered trauma?" Brianna asks.

"Yes. Trauma could also be all those comments by people who assumed or suggested your dad was involved in a gang. Most people who experience trauma do not develop post-traumatic stress disorder (PTSD). Trauma is not necessarily one event. It can be the compounded experience of small events over and over. Kind of like death by a thousand cuts."

"So racism can be trauma . . . " Brianna says as she shakes her head. I nod.

How Stress Becomes Trauma

So, let's go back to our discussion about fight-flight-freeze for a moment. There you are, trying to escape a mountain lion that is interested in having you for dinner. If you are able to run away successfully, you stop running, your breath slows, causing your heart rate to slow down, and your nervous system starts to recalibrate and return to equilibrium as it recognizes you are safe. Or if you escape by "playing dead" and freezing, after the lion leaves, you shudder and shake and return back to your clan and your body recovers. Trauma occurs when your brain gets "stuck" in the stressful event and is not able to achieve allostasis. Therefore, it makes sense that the longer someone is undergoing the stress, the more difficult it is for your brain to work through it. This is one of the reasons that I reject the idea of the common narrative of "big T" versus "little T" trauma and instead prefer to look at trauma on a continuum that is impacted by a wide variety of factors. If you think back to the iceberg for a moment, the more issues you face because of system inequities, the more difficult it is going to be to create safety, and the more likely you are to have one of those events or experiences become traumatic for you.

Not all stressful events result in trauma, and an even lower proportion result in a PTSD diagnosis. However, it is important to understand that stress and trauma, though distinct, are located on the same continuum and can start with the same stressor.[1] Immediately after the event, child trauma psychiatrist Bruce Perry says, our brain works to restore equilibrium by "pushing us to have repetitive, small 'doses' of recall. It seeks to make a sensitized system develop tolerance." In order to do this your brain may replay what happened, you may dream about it, you may find yourself telling and retelling the same story. Children are known to reenact the events.[2] The stress becomes trauma when your brain is unable to process what happened. Therefore, trauma isn't as much about what happens to you as it is about your interpretation, understanding, and processing (or lack thereof) of it.

Trauma occurs when you feel as though you are helpless, incapable of taking care of yourself, or lacking control. In Martin Seligman's famous rat experiments, two rats were housed in separate cages. In the first cage, every time that rat pressed a lever to receive a meal, it would receive an electric shock. In the second cage, the rat got shocked only when the first rat pressed the lever, making the shocks unpredictable. Both animals experienced stress and suffered during these experiments, but it was the second rat who became demoralized. Even when the second rat was then switched to having control over the shock when his lever was pressed (like the first rat), he gave up on trying to prevent the shocks. This is called learned helplessness.[3] The same thing occurs in humans. As Bruce Perry states, "a predictable and controllable stressor actually causes less 'stress' on a system while tolerance increases . . . our brains are naturally pulled to make sense of trauma in a way that allows us to become tolerant to it . . . [and] have some mastery."[4] In other words, if your brain is unable to integrate what happened to you, your sense of self and perceptions of the world fundamentally change.

Your nervous system also changes and becomes even more sensitive to trauma and stress in the future. In its attempts to protect you from future danger, your body becomes hypervigilant and will expend extra energy (at a higher cost) to ensure your survival. This change can occur whether your conscious brain is aware of it or not. As Bessel van der Kolk says, "After trauma, the world is experienced with a different nervous system. The survivor's energy now becomes focused on suppressing inner chaos, at the expense of spontaneous involvement in their life. These attempts to maintain control over unbearable physiological reactions can result in a whole range of physical symptoms."[5]

If someone is held down, restricted, or not able to act in the way they want to, whether that was part of the trauma (like being pinned down during a rape) or what they had to do to survive (hiding during a home invasion) or something you have to do because of our cultural norms (refraining from talking back to your boss when they say something mean to you), when we are unable to act, it also makes the situation more likely to be traumatic. While the inability to take action was rare in our hunter-gatherer days, it is increasingly common in our modern world.

Trauma and Your Brain

Scientists often talk about how we can divide our brains into three separate brains, known as triune brain,[6] based on function:

- the reptilian brain (consisting of the brainstem and cerebellum)
  - ▷ responsible for vital functions (heart rate, breathing, body temperature, digestion, sleeping, etc.)
- the mammalian brain (consisting of the limbic system, which is the thalamus, hypothalamus, hippocampus, and amygdala)
  - ▷ responsible for fight or flight response, learning, memory, emotions, perceiving danger
- neocortex (consisting of the frontal, temporal, occipital, and temporal lobes)
  - ▷ responsible for thinking, cognition, sensory perceptions, etc.

As the reptilian brain name suggests, this part of our brain is the oldest, evolutionarily speaking, and occurs in all reptiles. The limbic system is second oldest and occurs in all mammals. Finally, the neocortex only exists in primates and only takes up about 30 percent of our brains. When we are first born, the only part of our brain that is online is our reptilian brain. Human brains do not reach full development until age twenty-five. The mammalian brain is extremely important when we discuss trauma. When we enter a situation that is dangerous, our thalamus processes information received by our senses, which then goes directly to the amygdala to interpret its significance. The amygdala is often referred to as the body's "smoke detector"[7] as it decides whether the sensory information the body receives is dangerous; if so, it triggers the hypothalamus to begin fight or flight.

If the amygdala decides the information is not a threat to your survival, the information goes to the medial prefrontal cortex (known as MPFC, which is a part of your neocortex) and consciously you are able to decide how to react. When the amygdala immediately activates the hypothalamus, you don't have consciousness of your reaction. This is why the MPFC is referred to by van der Kolk as your "watchtower." It allows us to view the situation from a bigger perspective and choose our response. However, "when that system breaks down, we become like conditioned animals: the moment we detect danger we automatically go into fight-or-flight mode."[8] When we endure a trauma, often our amygdala becomes hypersensitive to any type of danger and we lose the ability to regulate our body reaction. On the more severe end, this may look like constantly scanning a room, being easily startled by sounds, or recoiling from touch.

Since trauma affects the deeper and older areas of the brain, the ones that we are not conscious of, this is why it is critically important that trauma healing involves healing the reptilian and mammalian brain. It is critically important to teach your body how to feel safe again. This can be accomplished in different ways with yoga, mindfulness, exercise, breathing, safe touch, and newer therapies such as EMDR (Eye Movement Desensitization and Reprocessing) and Brainspotting. These therapies use bilateral stimulation to help you activate and reprocess trauma stored in the amygdala, which cannot be accessed through talking only. For more information, check out the resources at the back of this book. If you are reading these pages and recognizing that you have trauma, I cannot stress enough the importance of seeing a therapist to work through it.

Alcohol becomes a way to cope with the trauma. We use it to self-regulate and medicate ourselves to deal with our pain. It makes complete sense that we want to reach for something that is a depressant, like alcohol, to help us turn down the intensity of our brains and feel safe. There is nothing wrong with your desire to do that. However, it is important to note that the temporary relief causes more dysregulation in the long term. The more you drink, the more dysregulated you become and the more you teach yourself to disconnect from your body when stressed or triggered.

"Now that I think about it, I really changed after my dad died. Those words you said . . . too much, too soon, too fast . . . that really resonates," Brianna says slowly, taking everything in. "Like my dad's death, we didn't even have time to grieve. It was all too much." Tears start to trickle slowly down Brianna's face. She touches her cheeks, looking embarrassed, and reaches for a tissue. "I'm sorry," she mumbles as she blots her face.

"There is absolutely nothing to be sorry about," I say. "This is good. Keep going."

She inhales sharply. "Everything changed afterwards. My mom had to get another job to keep us going, we moved in with my grandparents, and my brother and I had to change schools. I hated my new school. My grandparents were old and a lot of the responsibility of caring for my brother fell on me."

"How did you feel during this?" I ask.

"Angry. But I never expressed that. Everyone was so devastated, I felt so powerless watching all the adults in my life fall apart. I thought, *I can't be mad, I have to take care of everyone.* But I was. I was pissed. It all felt so unfair. I had to grow up so fast. I didn't realize how much it affected me until now. Is that normal? Why am I just realizing this now?"

"It's really normal, Brianna," I say. "As a culture, we do not often talk about how common trauma is. We often believe trauma only happens to people who are abused or veterans. We often resist thinking of ourselves as enduring trauma because we fear we won't be able to heal."

Brianna nods, as a fresh wave of tears rushes down her cheeks. Our session is ending.

"This is really good," I say. "I think this is going to help us understand why you drink on a deeper level. As you go about the rest of your week, I want you to notice how you think about your dad, and what happened. See if you can notice who you were before your dad died and how you changed after. And notice if there is still anger there."

"Okay, I can do that." Brianna stands up and closes the door behind her.

Exercise: Grab a piece of paper and pen and write down your answers to these questions.

Before you dive in, if you know you have a trauma history or have been diagnosed with PTSD or complex post-traumatic stress disorder (CPTSD), it may not be helpful for you to explore this list alone or at all. Please note this list of questions is not exhaustive and not meant to provide a diagnosis of any kind. The only person who knows if they have trauma is you, and you are the only one who gets to decide if you want to use that word.

- Have you ever lost a parent, caregiver, or anyone close to you? If so, what was it like for you? What was your response to it? Do you notice any distinction between who you were before versus after (like Brianna realized)?
- Did your caregivers separate, get a divorce, or leave when you were growing up? What was that experience like for you?
- Have you endured any physical, sexual, or emotional abuse?

- Were you bullied as a kid? How did you deal with it?
- Did you grow up in a home that had domestic violence? Did you watch a loved one or parent experience sexual, physical, or emotional abuse?
- Have you experienced racism, sexism, harassment, homophobia, or discrimination?
- Do you have a disability or chronic illness or have you undergone any kind of medical trauma?
- Have you ever had a miscarriage or abortion or experienced infertility?
- Did you grow up in poverty? Were there nights you went to sleep at night not having enough to eat?
- Have you ever experienced discrimination from a medical provider or others because of the size of your body or how it looks?

Chapter 4

The Culture of Shame

**What we don't need in the midst of struggle
is shame for being human.**

—Brené Brown

"Okay, I'm a mess and I completely failed my homework assignment from last week." Tara kicks off her sandals and flops onto my couch dramatically before pulling her legs into a cross-legged position.

"Did you forget to do it?" I ask.

"No, I remembered. I'm just a giant asshole to myself."

I smile. "Well it sounds like you did the assignment then. You noticed it, and it seems like you haven't noticed this before."

"Oh, I figured I was supposed to stop doing that and I honestly just gave up because I'm a mess and I don't think that's going to change."

"You seem like you actually really cared about this assignment, Tara. It's . . . " I search for the right word, "refreshing."

Tara rolls her eyes and then darts them back at me. "Don't get used to it."

"What made this week different?"

"I don't know, just what we were talking about last week. I really didn't realize how much I beat myself up. It sucks. And I guess I was just thinking, for the first time in a while, what it would be like to be free from that."

"Ah, sounds like you experienced, dare I say, hope?" I say playfully. Tara tends to shut down if we get too serious, so I try to walk a balanced line to keep her from feeling too vulnerable.

"Yeah, yeah, something like that."

"So, your inner critic's voice . . . whose voice is that?" I ask.

"I'm not admitting to hearing voices, Amanda," she says sarcastically.

"Ha, I know," I say. "I mean, does your critic's voice sound like anyone you know."

"Mom." I tread slowly as this is a sensitive topic that we have not explored too much in our work together. I do know that since Tara's parents got divorced a year ago, she hasn't spoken to her mom, but their relationship began massively deteriorating when she came out as gay a year before that, at age twenty.

"What do you say to yourself that sounds like Mom?" I ask.

"That I'm never going to get better. I'm a loser for dropping out of school. I'm a slut. I'm wasting my life. I'm wasting my dad's money. It's pointless. I should stop trying and give up."

"What is it like to live in your head with those thoughts on repeat?"

"It really sucks. . . . But I don't really have much faith in being able to change this. It's just the way I think now. . . ." Tara trails off. "I just have done so much shit I'm not proud of, made so many mistakes. I don't know."

"That makes sense," I say, trying to reassure her. "Often the biggest barrier in changing is actually facing our mistakes and the parts of ourselves that we are running from."

Tara switches gears and returns to her sarcastic banter. We've appeared to hit her vulnerability threshold. "Well, ya know, crippling guilt and self-loathing, just another day in the life."

Understanding Shame

One of the most important things that I teach my clients in therapy is that there is a distinct difference between the emotions of guilt, shame, embarrassment, and humiliation. If you look up the definitions of these four words in the dictionary, there is a lot of overlap and confusion. I found one definition that defined shame as "a guilty and embarrassed feeling that you have when you or someone else behaves badly."[1] Umm, what? No wonder we are confused! Most commonly, people overuse the word "guilt" because they don't understand the difference between guilt and shame.* Case in point: Tara says she is in a perpetual state of guilt, but really she is in a shame spiral. The word "shame" often has an intense connotation to it compared to the word "guilt," so people refrain from using it. Let's break it down so we can talk about the differences.

Guilt is a feeling of unease or remorse after you have done something wrong, especially toward another person. We feel guilty when our behavior does not align with our values or morals. This is the critical difference between guilt and shame. Guilt is an emotion we feel based on our behavior, not based on our self-perceived worth as a human being. Of course, guilt can also become unhealthy. One of the most common ways this happens is when we feel guilty about imagined scenarios. For example, we can feel guilty about a scenario that

---

* Different mental health therapists, doctors, and researchers have different ideas about the differences. I most align with the model created by the research of June Price Tangney and Ronda L. Dearing. Brené Brown also follows this model and has done her own empirical research studies, which back this up as well.

has not happened yet or is unlikely to happen. We can feel a sense of guilt even at the idea of setting boundaries with a friend. Tara often experiences this when we discuss the possibility that she could try setting boundaries with her mom. It can also happen when we obsessively ruminate over our past mistakes and dissect and scrutinize everything we said and did (especially if we are trying to figure out if the person likes us or is upset with us). This is known as maladaptive guilt.

However, if we struggle with low self-worth and think poorly about ourselves, almost every mistake we make can become a source of shame rather than guilt. This is why dissecting these definitions is important; two people can make the same mistake, and one feels guilt while another feels shame. Specifically, though Tara describes herself as a "mess," one strength she identifies is time management. She never is late to our appointments. When she is late to a doctor's appointment, she reports feeling guilty for wasting the doctor's time, but she did not feel shame because she was a bad person for this.

From an evolutionary perspective, guilt can be helpful because it can propel us to take responsibility for our mistake, apologize, and change our behavior in the future. If you think back to Chapter 2, we are evolutionarily wired to cooperate with other humans and share. This reciprocal altruism is how we stayed alive and thrived in tribes for thousands of years. However, this also made us particularly interested in fairness and morality. When we cooperated and shared with others, it was important to not get screwed over. Thus, owning up to cheating or mistakes we made (in response to guilt) was likely evolutionarily advantageous, especially in order to avoid being embarrassed, shamed, or humiliated.

The emotion of guilt is distinct from shame, which Brené Brown describes as "the intensely painful feeling or experience of believing that we are flawed and therefore unworthy of love and belonging."[2] To put it simply, guilt says, "I made a mistake," while shame says, "I am a mistake." With shame, we internalize our behavior. Shame leads us to question our character and worth as a human being, while guilt has us question our behavior. As such, shame robs us of the ability of changing because we get stuck in believing "this is just who I am." The semantics of this may not seem important, but trust me, they are. Every time Tara relapses, she does not feel guilt when she drinks and goes on a bender, she feels intense shame. She uses the experience as evidence that she cannot change because she is "a slut and a mess" rather than recognizing that her actions are not in alignment with what she wants and working to change her behavior in the future. Furthermore, shame is so debilitating because it is rooted in the "fear of disconnection." On a physiological level, our body responds intensely to this threat, as being disconnected from others in hunter-gatherer days meant almost-certain death.

The words "humiliation" and "embarrassment" can also be easily confused with each other or with the concepts of shame and guilt. Embarrassment is the feeling of being nervous or self-conscious about what people think of you. It is often based on a mistake or a circumstance that is not permanent, and often a common experience that happens to others, which is why it is the least debilitating emotion out of shame, guilt, embarrassment, and humiliation.[3] Tara may have felt embarrassed the first few times she got drunk because this is often a common experience in our culture and something we laugh about with our friends. But now, after a few years of doing this, losing friends, and dropping out of college, it is no longer embarrassing for her, it's shameful.

Humiliation is the state of being in a painful loss of pride, self-respect, or dignity. It is often associated with being called out publicly or labeled a certain name based on your behavior. However, it does not necessarily mean that you believe what is being said about you. Tara may feel humiliation when someone calls her a junkie while she is in rehab, but not feel shame because she knows she doesn't do drugs. That word doesn't have a big impact on her. This is why, according to Brown's research, shame is a more destructive emotion for us to feel compared to humiliation.[4] Humiliation becomes shame when we internalize and believe it. Or as psychiatrist Donald Klein explains, "People believe they deserve their shame; they do not believe they deserve their humiliation."[5] However, the more often we are humiliated, the lower our self-worth. The more we respect and admire the person who is humiliating us, the more likely our humiliation becomes shame. Thus, children are especially susceptible to humiliation becoming shame.

Societal Shame

You may be thinking . . . okay I understand how shame is unhelpful for healing and changing my drinking habits, but isn't shame important for our society to function? Doesn't fear of being shamed make people more likely to follow rules and laws and behave in a socially acceptable manner? Let's pause for a second and define what is it to shame someone. Shaming someone involves name-calling, put-downs, ridiculing, or belittling. It focuses on the person's character and worth as a person rather than their behavior. This is important because, especially in today's social media call-out culture, you should understand that you can have shame arise *without being shamed*. Especially, as we talked about above, if you have low self-worth to begin with. Saying someone's behavior is bad or harmful is not the same thing as saying they are a bad person. The first is asking for accountability, the second is shaming.

So back to the question: Doesn't shame play an important role in societal stability? Brené Brown's research finds the opposite to

Emotion	Definition	Example	Think of Your Own Example
Guilt	The feeling of unease or remorse after you have done something wrong, especially toward another person	Tara feels guilty for being late to her doctor's appointment. She knows this is not like her and makes a plan to leave earlier in the future.	
Maladaptive Guilt	Involves obsessive rumination over a mistake or wrongdoing	Tara feels maladaptive guilt when she imagines setting boundaries with her mom.	
Shame	The feeling or experience of believing that we are flawed and therefore unworthy of love and belonging	Tara feels shame that she dropped out of college, has been to rehab numerous times, and keeps blacking out. She calls herself a loser.	
Embarrassment	The feeling of being nervous or self-conscious about what people think of you	Tara gets too drunk for the first time and feels embarrassed that she made a fool of herself. Her friends and she joke about this and move on.	
Humiliation	The painful loss of pride, self-respect, or dignity	Tara is called a "junkie" while she is in rehab by a girl she doesn't like and feels humiliated because she doesn't do drugs and is angry that this girl is trying to disrespect her like that.	

be true. She writes, "Shame is highly correlated with addiction, violence, aggression. . . . Researchers don't find shame correlated with positive outcomes at all—there are no data to support that shame is a helpful compass for good behavior." Given this research, I find it difficult to believe that it was evolutionarily advantageous to feel shame. Furthermore, even if it were to be, our brain's hardwiring is not set up to be able to have productive conversations with people we don't know intimately, let alone billions of them (over the internet). Remember, we are wired to only be connected to around 150 people maximum. This is one reason why social media and the internet are causing polarization among humans. Our brain wants to save energy, and when we do not know someone or have a relationship with them, we are quick to make a judgment about who they are based on a small piece of information we have. This is known as the Fundamental Attribution Error. Without context, we tend to revert to shaming and blaming others, especially with the computer screen between us. To deal with this intense shame and fear, we often discharge our shame by blaming others and seeking revenge in order to regain a semblance of power.

As I am writing this book in 2021, I am keenly aware of this polarization. With the collision of the COVID-19 pandemic, which further exposed the urgent need for racial and systemic equality, blame in politics, and fear in the news, polarization is at an all-time high. Our culture is driven by scarcity, and we constantly feel as though we do not have enough and aren't good enough as we compare ourselves to others. To be clear, I am not saying that everyone who is living in America right now has trauma, but almost everyone is dealing with stress at an extremely high level. Marginalized groups of people, especially Black, Indigenous, and People of Color (BIPOC), are more prone to develop trauma as they are more likely to have been sick, had loved ones die of COVID, lost their jobs and health insurance, and experience a higher level of anxiety with the concern that they could lose basic rights. Women, especially mothers, have taken on a huge load during the pandemic. A recent study states that heavy drinking among women rose by 41 percent since the pandemic began in March 2020,[6] and alcoholic liver disease among women is up 30 percent over the last year, says Dr. Jessica Mellinger, a liver specialist at University of Michigan.[7]

The Connection Between Shame and Trauma

Shame and trauma are inextricably linked. Since the hallmark of trauma is feeling powerless to stop what is happening to you, shame immediately sprouts up as a way for your brain to make sense of it. Shame is the feeling that arises that tells us, "I am a bad person and it's my fault this happened. If I would have done or said this, I could have prevented it. I should have been able to." I have never met anyone who has been through trauma, especially a woman, who has not developed shame and blamed herself in the process. Bessel van der Kolk echoes this sentiment. "Deep down many traumatized people are even more haunted by the shame they feel about what they themselves did or did not do under the circumstances. They despise themselves for how terrified, dependent, excited or enraged they felt."[8] Shame is the fear of disconnection. If we have been through something traumatic, most of us think that if someone were to find out, they would not want a relationship with us. So, what do we do to prevent that from happening? We hide our trauma. We pretend it didn't happen, don't talk about it, and judge ourselves for the experience. This breeds shame.

As Brené Brown discovered in her research, shame requires three ingredients to survive: secrecy, silence, and judgment.[9] The more we hide and don't talk about it, the worse the shame as well as the effects of the trauma can become. Research on survivors of rape indicates that covering up and hiding what happened can cause more harm to survivors than the actual event.[10] Survivors of trauma feel this way regardless of how innocent an outsider would deem them, often citing others as having trauma that is more legitimate than theirs. For example, women who are sexually assaulted typically say they don't feel they have trauma because they weren't raped, individuals who were emotionally or physically abused by family often say their experience wasn't that bad because they knew and loved the person who hurt them, and individuals who witness violence tend to think they shouldn't be affected because they weren't the victim of it. So if you feel shame about something that has happened to you that you wouldn't blame a friend for, it is likely you have been through a traumatic incident.

I often use an umbrella metaphor to describe the connection among shame, addiction, and trauma. If trauma is the hail that rains down on us, we use an umbrella in order to protect ourselves from feeling the pain of it. The umbrella includes all the maladaptive coping skills that we develop in order to deal with the trauma. Though we are specifically talking about alcohol use in the concept of this book, we can also interchange this with other methods of numbing and coping such as drug use, dieting, eating disorders, perfectionism, excessive exercising, shopping, addictive relationships, gambling, and busyness to name a few. (If you struggle with your alcohol use, it is also very likely you may have other maladaptive coping skills from this list that you fall into as well, or at the very least you are more likely to fall into those after you change your relationship with drinking. We will discuss that more in part 3.)

These behaviors are also what are on the surface and therefore seen by others and identified as the problem, when in reality, they are merely symptoms of the deeper issue, such as unprocessed trauma, shame, and pain. I often say that shame is a binding and freezing emotion that shows up in the body much like the freeze response does in trauma. It makes it difficult to feel the other emotions that are going on. We get stuck in thinking about how we are to blame for our problems or what we could have done differently to prevent the trauma from happening. However, in order to get to the root of our issues, we have to be willing to work through our shame and face the pain underneath.

Trauma

Mental Health Issues   Ableism
Sexual Abuse   Racism   Gaslighting
Death of Loved Ones   Social Isolation   Bullying
Emotional Neglect   Sexism   Poverty   Parentification
Abandonment   Divorce   Job Loss   Miscarriages   Heterosexism
Divorce   Medical Trauma   Harassment   Injury   Chronic Illness
Scapegoating   Insomnia   Discrimination   Ageism   Weight Stigma
Violence   Sexual Assault   Invalidation   Infertility   Physical Abuse

Gambling   Dieting
Shopping   Drug Use
Alcohol Use   Eating Disorders
Excessive Exercise   Perfectionism
Relationships & Sex   Workaholism & Busyness

Feelings of
Pain

Feelings of
Shame

Shame is even more common among those of us who have alcohol use disorders, as the effects of alcohol make it likely that we have put ourselves in risky situations and/or done things we regret. In these situations, we of course feel it is absolutely our fault if we end up in a traumatic situation. This is exacerbated by the fact that morality is so intertwined with alcohol and drug use (despite the positive push toward destigmatizing addiction and calling it a disease). Therefore, individuals close to us often blame and shame us for engaging in this risky behavior, thinking it will help us stop. When I worked at a rehab, the most common thing I had to teach parents and partners was to stop shaming their loved ones who were struggling with substance use disorders. Parents truly believed if they shamed their kids enough, they would be able to get them to get sober. They were blown away when I told them their loved one already thinks the absolute worst about themselves. They thought they were helping, but berating them only adds fuel to the fire and makes them more likely to use drugs or drink in order to escape that pain.

Even when loved ones were able to stop, it is difficult for those of us with substance use disorders to stop beating ourselves up for the harm we have caused others and ourselves. We may feel as though we "deserve it" and want to punish ourselves. However, we can only sit in extreme shame and self-loathing for so long before our brain naturally seeks a break. Often we end up drinking more or engaging in other maladaptive coping skills to numb this pain and escape it. The irony of this, of course, is that this often leads us right back to the same behavior that led us to drink in the first place, creating a cycle of self-sabotage. If we are looking to break free from our self-sabotaging behavior, we must be willing to work through the shame. **Shame is the glue that holds self-sabotage in place.**

The Cycle of Self-Sabotage

As we discussed in Chapter 3, safety is a crucial element to recovery from a traumatic incident. Until we are able to be in an environment that is safe and we are able to cultivate safety in our bodies, healing is not possible. We do this by attempting to control our environment. This may manifest in a number of different ways: by being hypervigilant and constantly scanning our environment for our abuser, or not leaving our house during certain times of day, or avoiding certain situations altogether. Another way we may accomplish this is by using alcohol or another addictive behavior in order to control our emotions and numb ourselves so we don't have to feel our pain. The other thing our brain tries to do in order to process the trauma and integrate the experience is to desensitize itself to what happened. Your brain may do this in a few different ways: thinking about it, talking about it, dreaming about it, or even . . . reenacting it. This is where self-sabotage comes in.

In Bruce Perry's research with traumatized children, especially those in the foster care system, he noticed that these children would often present in a calm manner when they first arrived at new foster homes, but later self-sabotage by acting defiantly. They do this unconsciously as a way to create predictability for themselves. They know how to handle chaos, so rather than allowing someone else to abandon them, they will act defiantly as a way to be in control of their abandonment. Adults do the same thing. Ever broken up with someone out of fear that they were going to break up with you later? Didn't prepare for a job interview out of fear of being rejected? Started an argument with someone to avoid telling them how you feel? As Virginia Satire famously stated, "Most people prefer the certainty of misery to the misery of uncertainty."

Self-sabotaging behavior specifically shows up after a traumatic event as a way for your brain to reenact what happened and reprocess it. Since the hallmark of trauma is not having power and control over the situation, when we reenact it, we often do it in a way that allows our brains to feel in control of the situation. Bruce Perry describes how children often literally reenact what happened to them in therapy. If they were physically abused, they act that out, or if they were called names, they will repeat words that were said to them as a way to (unconsciously) desensitize themselves to their memories and create a tolerance. Perry states:

> Our brains are naturally pulled to make sense of trauma in a way that allows us to become tolerant to it, to mentally shift the traumatic experience from one in which we are completely helpless to one in which we have some mastery. . . . [The patient's] brain was trying, through reenactment, to make the trauma into something predictable and hopefully, ultimately, boring.[11]

This specific phenomenon explains why when individuals experience sexual abuse (especially if they are children), it is common for them to develop hypersexuality or hyposexuality as a way to cope with what happened.[12] Hypersexuality is the equivalent to your brain reenacting what happened again but from a position of power, while hyposexuality is regaining control by avoiding the trigger altogether. I bring this up because this phenomenon of being sexually assaulted and then becoming promiscuous is extremely common among women with substance use disorders. One in four women in the United States has an experience with sexual assault. On college campuses, 90 percent of rapes and at least 50 percent of sexual assaults involve alcohol.[13]

This makes those of us who drink more than our friends even more likely to have an experience with sexual assault.

Trauma leads us to believe that what happened to us is our fault, and shame robs us of our ability to change our response to trauma. When you bring those two things together, it is not a surprise that so many individuals who experience trauma do not believe they are capable or worthy of changing. This leads them to beat themselves up and stay stuck in the cycle of self-sabotage because when life is constantly knocking you down, it sometimes feels better to be doing the knocking to yourself. As painful as that may be, at least you know you are in control over it.

"Wait, wait, wait. So, you mean to tell me that my slutty-ness is a response to shame?" Tara's eyes look like they are going to pop out of her head.

"Yup!" I say. "Exactly."

"Damn," Tara says in disbelief.

Make a mistake, engage in unhealthy behavior; compare ourselves to our society's high ideals

Cycle of Shame

Become overwhelmed; act out or self-numb in order to cope with shame

Feel shame and beat yourself up; "there's something wrong with me"

Resolve to change; set an unrealistic goal

"And you beating yourself up is also a response to shame," I add.

"What do you mean?" Tara asks.

"Well, humans cannot tolerate too much self-loathing before we snap and either numb that pain or rebel against it. For a lot of us, drinking or any other addictive behavior becomes this unhealthy cycle of the escape we need and then the punishment we believe we deserve."

Tara is silent for a moment and I can tell she is deep in thought. She says, "I've never thought of this before, but I do punish myself by drinking. It's like I twist the knife on myself. I think I deserve to be hungover."

"Yup, that makes sense. And the meaner you are to yourself, the more deeply you get stuck in this cycle."

"I guess I should probably stop beating myself up," Tara says.

"I'd say so. But here's the trap. You also can't beat yourself up for beating yourself up," I say with a wink.

"OMG, I can't with you today!" Tara says half joking, but I can tell based on her expression that this session really opened her eyes and gave her a lot to think about.

I know for myself when I learned that my promiscuity was actually a trauma response to being raped, it cracked the shame shell that strangled me. I'm hoping it can do the same for you. We covered a lot of heavy topics in this chapter, so I invite you to pause and take a breath. Check in with your body and your breath. Take a break if you need to before diving into the exercise. If you are not sure whether you struggle with shame or not, below is a list that may help you connect some of the dots for yourself.

You May Struggle with Shame Because . . .

- Your family stressed the importance of accomplishments, leading you to believe that productivity determines your worth

- You were raised in a religion that used shame
- You have been verbally, sexually, physically, or emotionally abused
- Your family often criticized, judged, or compared you to others
- You were neglected or bullied while growing up
- Your family kept secrets and/or encouraged you to hide things or lie
- You were raised in an environment where parental figures were overly concerned with your or their appearance or with your family's reputation

Chapter 5

Our Bodies, Ourselves . . . and Alcohol

We are hypervigilant about everything we put into our body, everything we do to our body . . . and we drink fucking rocket fuel.
—Holly Whitaker

"So, how have things been?" I ask Andrea. She is about two weeks into an experiment of not drinking alcohol for thirty days.

"Honestly, I'm sick of it," she says with a sigh.

"Okay, what's been going on?"

"Well, I mean it hasn't really been hard or anything. It's not like I'm *craving* alcohol." She uses air quotes around this. "I just feel like my life is boring. Like you asked me the question, would your life be better if I didn't drink. And honestly, I feel like no, it hasn't been."

"I understand that." I pause. "I think it's also important to remember that it has only been two weeks. I think some of the positive outcomes of not drinking take some time to show up. Of course, you can always choose to forgo this experiment."

"You know I'm not going to; I don't just quit things," Andrea says proudly.

"I know. And for the record, I wouldn't consider this to be quitting. That's why I used the word 'forgo,'" I say with a smile.

"Forgo is a fancy word for quitting."

"Fair enough," I say. "Tell me why you feel like not drinking has not made your life better."

"Well, I just honestly feel more anxious and disconnected from my classmates. Like I already feel a bit disconnected from them because I'm a little bit older and am engaged. And with my mom having cancer, I feel so much older than I am sometimes. So now that I haven't been drinking, I feel so awkward at our happy hours. It's like I've forgotten how to socialize. Going out once or twice a week was the one thing that really helped me forget my responsibilities, it helped me feel normal. Now I just have another reason to not fit in."

"I understand," I say. "What is it like to feel like you don't fit in?"

"It sucks. I mean I'm used to it; I have felt like I didn't belong since moving here at age nine. I barely could speak English. My parents were not great at it obviously. Thankfully I learned quickly because I was the one that had to translate everything to my parents and even help my sister. Since I was younger than my sister, I picked up English way quicker."

"That makes sense," I say.

"So yeah, growing up I was the weird one with parents who didn't speak English. I don't want to be the weird one that doesn't drink."

"Were people weird with you when you didn't drink with them at happy hour?"

"I mean I felt awkward but not really. But I also think that's only because I made an excuse that I had to get up really early that morning to train for the ten-mile race I signed up for. I just think that humans have been drinking alcohol forever. It's healthy in moderation and I think trying to stop drinking weirdly makes me want to drink more."

"I get that," I say. "That can be something that happens during an experiment like this. But I do want to debunk some myths about alcohol. . . . "

Early Alcohol Consumption

Although alcohol is widely consumed throughout the world, it's helpful to understand its origins and how this came to be. Just because something is widely adapted does not always mean that it is healthy or positive for society. As we talked about in the last two chapters, it is clear that a lot of what modern society considers normal is not a match for our evolutionary hardwiring. So, what about alcohol?

Let's take a trip back to early hunter-gatherer days. When did humans first start consuming alcohol? It is believed that the first alcohol was consumed by our ancestors in the form of rotting fruit. As long as the fruit has a high enough sugar content and there is wild yeast, fermentation occurs and produces ethanol, with an alcohol content of up to 5 percent (equivalent to the amount of alcohol in an average beer today). The earliest traces of an alcoholic beverage (a type of wine made from rice and honey) were found in China around 7000–5600 BC.[1]

Once human beings began to settle on land and farm, they were able to harvest crops and eventually discovered how to make wine and beer. While initially it is believed to have been only consumed during celebratory or religious occasions, by the sixteenth century, due to frequent water contamination, most European doctors recommended that individuals drink beer and wine instead of water.[2] Soon after, the consumption of alcohol in humans dramatically changed with the invention and mainstream production of distilled spirits. As a result, numerous countries attempted to regulate, tax, and curb

' drinking as people began to suspect that drunkenness
_d crime rates and disarray. Most religious leaders were
specifically against the consumption of spirits, which led to the temperance movement in 1820. The movement's biggest accomplishment
(and then downfall) was the ratification of the Eighteenth Amend-
ment in 1919, beginning a period known as Prohibition. Two years
after the end of Prohibition in 1935, Alcoholics Anonymous was
formed.

The Alcohol Education You Didn't Get in School

I probably could write an entire chapter on the effects that alcohol
has on our minds and bodies and there are entire books written about
it. As a society, it seems we learn about every study that finds an issue
with the food we eat, and yet we don't learn about what alcohol does
to our bodies. As Holly Whitaker says, alcohol is the same chemical
compound as rocket fuel.[3] Many people think that it is natural because it is produced through fruit or wheat (wine or beer). That's true
for some types of alcohol. However, it's also important to remember
that your body considers alcohol to be a poison. And there are many
"natural" things that are poisonous for humans.

Contrary to popular belief, even one serving of alcohol impacts
your body. In 2020 a global study confirmed that there is no safe
amount of alcohol consumption that is good for your health.[4] Though
I am not sure that sentiment has trickled down to mainstream media
yet. We may know a lot about the impacts that heavy drinking has on
our bodies, like liver disease and cancer. But not much is said about
the short-term effects, the impact of having a single serving of alcohol.
Let's break this down.

The second alcohol is ingested, your body is looking to get rid of it
as soon as possible. To do this, your digestive system halts the regular

digestion of food in order to start metabolizing alcohol. It essentially fast-tracks digesting alcohol so it can get rid of it in your liver. As you can imagine, this majorly disrupts digestion, and your body's ability to derive nutrients from the food you consume while drinking. This is why alcohol consumption is linked to bloating, constipation, diarrhea, loose stools, cramping, and headaches.[5] Digestion also gets disrupted when alcohol destroys good bacteria in your gut, causing unhealthy bacteria to flourish and messing up the ratio of good versus bad bacteria (a condition called dysbiosis). This matters because the bacteria in your gut produce neurochemicals that your brain uses to produce serotonin and other neurotransmitters. In fact, scientists report that gut bacteria are responsible for producing over 95 percent of the brain's serotonin.[6] Alcohol also messes with our blood sugar balance as the liver has to stop doing its job of producing glucose and other hormones that regulate our blood sugar levels. If you also have a habit of not eating much while drinking, you are even more likely to exhibit low blood sugar.[7] Over time, heavy drinkers can develop hypoglycemia.

If you drink alcohol faster than your body can break it down and metabolize it, this causes further issues, such as broken capillaries and cancers. This is because your body is incapable of breaking down ethanol, so it turns it into acetaldehyde, a highly toxic substance that can destroy cellular tissue, before breaking it down.[8] The World Health Organization classifies acetaldehyde as a Class 1 Human Carcinogen.[9] Since acetaldehyde is highly toxic, your body does not want to store it. The alternative solution is to release it through oxidation. In order to do this, your blood vessels have to expand, which can burst capillaries. This is the reason that alcohol can show up through your breath and sweat. Sometimes your body is still not able to keep up and get rid of acetaldehyde through oxidation, so it stays in your system. Alcohol has been linked to cancer (especially in the intestines and esophagus), strokes, and Alzheimer's disease.[10] Breast cancer is specifically linked to drinking. Over a four-year period, one study found that women increase their risk of breast cancer by 15 percent if they drink three alcoholic beverages a week, and it increases by 10 percent with each additional drink they have after that.[11]

Many people use alcohol as a sleep aid, but the truth is having even one serving of alcohol completely disrupts your sleep. While it appears to make you fall asleep faster, sleep expert Matthew Walker says, "Alcohol sedates you out of wakefulness, but it does not induce natural sleep. The electrical brainwave state you enter via alcohol is not that of natural sleep; rather, it is akin to a light form of anesthesia."[12] Thus, you are not actually falling asleep faster, you are simply experiencing sedation. According to Walker, alcohol-induced sleep is not restful for two reasons. First, it disrupts your sleep or "fragments" it, though this is often subtle enough to be unobservable by the individual experiencing it. Second, alcohol completely prevents your body from entering the most restful and important type of sleep, REM sleep. REM sleep is crucial for learning, as during this part of the sleep cycle, your brain transfers short-term memories into your long-term memory. And remember, it takes your body a few days to completely rid itself of alcohol. Therefore, you can experience a disruption in your sleep even a day or so after drinking alcohol. As a result, there is no healthy amount of alcohol due to its tremendous impacts on sleep,[13] although of course the impact on your body and mind varies depending on how much you drink.

How Alcohol Affects Your Mental Health

Now let's talk about how alcohol impacts your mental health. According to a new study, no amount of alcohol is safe for your brain. After studying the brains of over 25,000 participants, the researchers found that alcohol can create up to a 0.8 percent reduction in gray matter over time.[14] Gray matter is critically important for memory, muscle control, emotional regulation, and sensory perception. While 0.8 percent may seem like an inconsequential figure, it is four times the amount that smoking impacts your brain. Lead researcher of the study Anya Topiwala says, "There is no threshold drinking for harm—any alcohol is worse. Pretty much the whole brain seems to be affected—not just specific areas as previously thought."[15]

Like all other drugs, alcohol is an artificial chemical that stimulates the pleasure receptors in your brain. Since it is an artificial high, and your brain wants to retain homeostasis, it produces chemicals such as dynorphin to reduce the intensity of the sensation over time.[16] This is known as tolerance and is the reason why you need to drink more alcohol over time to experience the same effects. However, this chemical pathway also reduces the individual's ability to find joy in non-alcohol- or drug-related pleasures.[17] Therefore, drinking actually negatively impacts your mental health by making your life and ordinary moments, which are often cited as the key to living a fulfilling life, less pleasurable.

Although alcohol is a depressant, it's important to remember that your body is always looking to be in homeostasis. Thus, when you ingest a depressant, your body produces cortisol and adrenaline (often associated with anxiety) in order to counteract the effects of alcohol and bring your body back into balance. As addiction neuroscientist Judith Grisel explains, "The states of withdrawal and craving from any drug are always exactly opposite to the drug's effects. If a drug makes you feel relaxed, withdrawal and craving are experienced as anxiety or tension."[18] Your body experiences withdrawal even when it is not physically addicted to the drug. This word simply defines the process of detoxification as your body rids itself of what it ingested and returns to homeostasis. If you struggle with anxiety or use alcohol as a way to relieve stress, you are going to end up with more stress and anxiety the following day than you started with. Drinking doesn't alleviate your anxiety. It sedates you to its impact, and then the next day you are left with the same worries plus additional anxiety from the hormones your body produces in order to detox from the alcohol you consumed. This isn't even mentioning the fact that it's really difficult to take care of your mental health and build self-worth if you are continuously acting in ways that are out of alignment with your values when you drink.

Costs and Payoffs

"How did I not learn about these negative impacts of alcohol? Why don't they cover this in med school?" Andrea asks after I share some information about alcohol, how it is impacting her sleep (she struggles with insomnia) and anxiety.

"It's really not talked about enough," I say. "Do you feel any differently after learning about this?"

"I mean I'm still not thrilled at the idea of not drinking. And I'm not making any promises, but I do feel a little better about this thirty-day break. If nothing else, I am interested in seeing how it affects my sleep."

"That's great, Andrea. I also have an assignment I think may help you with this too." Andrea grabs her therapy notebook and looks up at me. "I want you to create a list of payoffs and costs of not drinking."

"Do you mean like pros and cons?"

"Kind of, but not quite. Pros and cons insinuate good and bad things. Instead, I want you to think about how everything we do has payoffs, or things we get from doing them, and costs, things we lose.

Even things we like to do may cost us money for example, but we get enjoyment out of them so they may be worth it."

"Okay," she says. "I'll see you next week."

In terms of evolution, there is a cost and a payoff to everything we do. Foraging for food costs us less energy than hunting and was less risky, but the payoff of getting a bear was worth it when we were successful. Often when we are struggling with changing a habit, it is because we don't realize the payoff we get from *not* changing. For example, maybe you are miserable at your current job and you want a new one, but you have not been able to get yourself to apply. There is likely a hidden payoff you are getting from not applying and staying where you are. For example, even if you are miserable, it is probably easier and takes less energy to stay at the same job. You may also be protecting yourself from the possibility of getting rejected and not being able to find a new job, so it's easier to not put yourself out there than to fail.

After learning everything you did in this chapter about alcohol's impact on your body, make a list of costs and payoffs for drinking and not drinking. It's important to note that whenever we are struggling to make a decision, we have a few options. We can try to change (quitting drinking or taking a break from it), continue with the status quo (keep drinking), or not make a decision right now. If you are in the third camp, you have every right to be there. Being on the fence is a perfectly reasonable place to be, and I think it's important to recognize that is a decision too. I am not a fan of trying to force yourself to make a decision. There is no rush. If you truly are not sure, no problem. At the same time, it's important to acknowledge that sitting on a fence can be quite uncomfortable. The list-making exercise below can help you get off the fence and make a decision before we go into part 2 of the book.

Continuing to Drink

Costs	Payoffs
-	-
-	-
-	-
-	-
-	-
-	-
-	-
-	-
-	-
-	-
-	-
-	-

Not Continuing to Drink

Costs	Payoffs
-	-
-	-
-	-
-	-
-	-
-	-
-	-
-	-
-	-
-	-
-	-
-	-

Part 2

The Tools You Need to Heal Your Relationship with Alcohol

Chapter 6

Reparenting Yourself

A woman becomes a responsible parent when
she stops being an obedient daughter.

—Glennon Doyle

"Reparenting?" Andrea looks at me dumbfounded. "I don't understand what you mean."

"We don't have to use that term," I say, "but one of the most important things we can do in therapy is honestly assess what skills and ideas our parents taught us about growing up, coping with life, and becoming an adult, and also where we may have gaps." I pause. "Often people fill gaps with coping methods like alcohol use or other unhealthy patterns."

"I get that. But I just don't feel like this applies to me. My parents were very involved—too involved—when I was growing up. They probably overparented me."

I smile. "And what was that like?"

"Well, I think intense is probably the best way to describe it. My mom was intense, my dad was intense. There was a lot of pressure on me to be perfect and prove that I had a right to be here and to take full advantage of the education system in America."

"Can you give me an example?"

"They would always say how lucky I was to be able to go to school in America. That it was an incredible opportunity. Even compared to my sister, I was the lucky one—to be able to immigrate here when I was younger, so English came easier to me than anyone in our family. If I ever didn't get an A my parents would act like I was throwing away the huge sacrifice they made in giving up everything to come to America. I feel like I'm always trying to make them proud."

"Do you not think they are proud of you?"

"I mean I think they are, but it doesn't feel like enough. I'm in med school, yeah that's great but I have a long way to go."

"Hmm," I say, "sounds like you may struggle with some perfectionism."

"Oh yeah. It wasn't just grades. I became pretty superstitious in high school too. It felt like if I was perfect enough, things would be okay. I remember one time I missed the bus for school in middle school and my mom lost her job later that day and I felt like it was my fault. After that I became obsessed with being perfect. And there was a lot of expectations from my parents because they said we were so lucky to have the opportunity to grow up in America. I was expected to help around the house, be at the top of my class, and be a star track athlete. I think because their English wasn't that good, they were really focused on tangible things—report cards, track meet rankings, it was how they were able to know I was doing well. But I guess it was good because I have a really good work ethic. I don't think I would be where I am if my parents didn't instill that in me."

"I think it definitely taught you how to work hard. But I wonder what else you learned from their reactions if you didn't perform well or didn't meet their expectations. We learn a lot from our parents not just from what they say, but from what they don't say and how they react if we don't meet their expectations."

"Well, my parents were very religious . . . Catholic. There was a lot of talk about sin and how God was always watching. So, if I got a bad grade or fought with my sister there was a lot of talk about how God was disappointed. My parents were also very concerned about my reputation. I got into a private school with a scholarship, and my mom was always concerned that people would think I got in just because I was Peruvian. I know my parents faced backlash of Americans saying foreigners were stealing their jobs. So, my parents were hyper aware of this and used to say that I had to be twice as good to prove myself."

"How did that feel?" I ask.

"I mean I was able to prove myself. I worked hard and graduated at the top of my class in high school. Got a full ride to UVA. It felt good for a while. My parents were proud of me. I know that. . . . But when I went abroad in college, it was like something in me snapped." Andrea shakes her head.

"What do you mean?"

"When I went abroad to Italy, it was the first time in my life when I actually felt fully free from them. Not that I want to be free or not talk to them . . ." Andrea stammered, "that sounds bad. I just mean that I felt freedom. I could be who I wanted to be, and nobody there knew my parents."

"What did your drinking look like when you were abroad?"

"It was the first time I could legally drink, so it was fun to drink wine with my friends, especially at restaurants. School was also a joke there, and my parents didn't really know what my grades were for the first time ever. That was so liberating. We went out to bars and clubs on the weekends and traveled to other cities. We were also in other countries, so the culture was foreign to all of us abroad. We all had to stumble through Italian and learn how to get around Rome. Ironically, being in a different country made me feel like I belonged more than I ever have. Sometimes it still feels like a dream . . . like that wasn't actually my life."

"It must have been hard to adjust when you came back," I say.

"Yeah, it was definitely hard adjusting to having less freedom again. I felt suffocated. I definitely drank more when I came back. Not like more when I was going out necessarily, but I had turned twenty-one and had gotten used to being able to buy alcohol for myself in Italy. Once I was back, whenever I felt suffocated, it was nice to be able to take the edge off with some drinks."

"Needing to be perfect all the time sounds exhausting. It makes sense that you would look for a bit of relief outside yourself."

"Yeah, well weirdly, being perfect felt easy in the beginning. I knew exactly how to win my parents' praises. I remember feeling like it was so easy. Just say yes and do what they say whether you agree or like it or not. I remember my sister struggling so much and fighting with them, where I just said yes. I felt like I discovered this secret. Say yes and everyone will like you. But then as life got more complicated in college, it became harder to control everything," Andrea says as she rubs her temples.

"Why do you think it was so important to you to avoid conflict?" I ask.

"I don't know," she says, "I just hate it, always have."

"So, before you learned to control things and say yes, do you remember how your parents reacted if you said no or disagreed with them?"

"Well, I learned to say yes to them about everything when I was pretty young, like in middle school. But actually, I do remember being in like first grade . . . " Andrea trailed off. "This is probably dumb," she says.

"Maybe," I say. "But these small moments can also reveal a pattern of how we learned to cope with challenges. Of course, a first grader's challenge may be different than an adult's, but it was probably significant to you at the time, which means it matters."

"Okay, yeah," Andrea says, understanding. "So anyway, I was in first grade and my mom wouldn't let me wear the outfit I had picked out for the first day of school. Looking back, I think she didn't want me to draw attention to myself. Modesty was very intertwined with their religion. Don't draw attention to yourself. I was so upset. I wanted to at least wear this sparkly purple headband, but she said no, '*porque yo lo dije*' . . . because I said so. She always said that."

I nod. Andrea continues, "I snuck the headband in my backpack and put it on when I got there. I forgot to take it off when I came home and she pulled it off my head. She was so angry at me. I remember her saying, 'You will never publicly disrespect me like that again.' Respect of elders is a big thing in Peruvian culture."

"How do you think that impacted you?"

"Well, I never insisted on picking out my clothes again if that's what you mean. But I also became a total teacher's pet. And the more my teacher Mrs. Garrison praised me, the more my mom praised me too."

"It sounds like it became very important for your mom to approve of you."

Andrea got quiet. "Yes. I feel like I'm still afraid of her sometimes . . . afraid of disappointing her."

"Let me ask you," I say, "did your parents ever model healthy conflict?"

"Oh God no. Everything was very hush hush in my house growing up. My parents don't really show their emotions. My mom used to say '*las emociones se sienten, no se ven*,' which means emotions are meant to be felt, not seen. I used to hear her crying in her room sometimes, but I never actually saw it in front of me. I never saw them fight, but I know there was often tension between them. I guess that's good. . . . I know it's unhealthy to have fighting in your house growing up."

"That is true. It can negatively impact kids if they constantly see their parents in unhealthy fights. However, it sounds like your parents sweep a lot of things under the rug, which is also unhealthy," I say, cautiously.

"Yeah, that's true," Andrea says, thinking.

"What do you think you may have learned about emotions from your parents?"

Andrea shakes her head. "I don't know. Honestly emotions were not something we really talked about. I remember one of my friends died when I was fifteen. She was killed by a drunk driver. It was pretty terrible. I remember being hysterical when I found out. All I wanted was my mom to sit next to me on the couch and rub my back and she . . . couldn't. She couldn't sit still. She kept getting up and cleaning and telling me to be grateful I wasn't in the car."

I shake my head and soften my gaze. "That sounds really difficult."

"The death or my mom's reaction?" Andrea asks.

"Both," I say.

"Yeah. I honestly think her reaction impacted me more. I remember thinking to myself, *I'm not sharing how I feel with you again.* And now that I think of it, soon after that is when my obsession with being perfect really took off."

Andrea's story tells me three important things about her. One—
Andrea never learned how to regulate her emotions. With the intensity of their expectation, her parents did not model healthy emotional
regulation. Emotions weren't talked about or openly displayed, and it
seems her mom may have tried to force gratitude on Andrea or solve
her problems when she shared her feelings. This was not because Andrea's parents weren't good parents; this is because Andrea's grandparents didn't teach her parents how to do this. (Which makes sense.
Remember, psychology and therapy were only established in the 1950s
and emotional intelligence as a concept was not created until 1990.)
This is only intensified because Andrea doesn't have many memories
of Peru and therefore fully identifies as American. However, her parents primarily identify with their Peruvian culture.

As a result, Andrea has had to manage conflicting expectations of
her parents with her peers. Andrea doesn't quite fit in with either culture completely, having a different experience from both her peers and
parents. This is exacerbated in Andrea's case because her sister is older
than her. While other third-culture kids have siblings that are also in
the same position, Andrea's sister was six years older than her, struggled to learn English, and identified more with their parents' culture.
This placed even more of a burden on Andrea to succeed and "take
advantage of the American Dream." As a result, Andrea never learned
how to cope with her emotions, process them, and use them to guide
her choices in life.

Two—Andrea was not given space to disagree with her parents or
have differing opinions. As a result, she learned to say yes to them in
order to get praise and avoid punishment. This likely resulted in her
inability to say no or authentically share how she feels, which is why
she struggles with boundaries at work, with her friends, and with her
fiancé. Andrea is afraid of conflict because she has little experience

with productive disagreements. Her parents never modeled boundary setting or healthy conflict in their own relationship, and she was dismissed by them if she shared a differing opinion or tried to advocate for herself. Her parents are highly influenced by their Peruvian culture, which very much believes in traditional gender roles and the importance of respecting one's elders (which in Andrea's case, looked like not being able to disagree with her parents).

Three—Andrea was taught that her worth was tied to how well she performed and what other people thought of her. Her parents were very concerned with trying to fit in and with how others perceived them. This led Andrea to become obsessed with being perfect as a way to cope with life and its challenges. She learned to put everyone before herself and ignore her own thoughts, opinions, and feelings. This approach appeared to work until she returned from being abroad, where she had had a taste of freedom and authenticity, and struggled to return to her old way of coping. She seems to have started using alcohol as a way to smooth that transition.

One thing as a therapist I know for sure is that we repeat what we don't repair. Sadly, our schools do not provide emotional education for children or teach them how to communicate, set boundaries, and engage in healthy conflict. Therefore, most of us need reparenting to teach ourselves some of the important coping skills that our parents missed. That's what this section is all about.

What Is Reparenting?

Reparenting has become a bit of a buzzword. It was first used by psychologists in reference to individuals who had childhood trauma and lacked secure attachment to a parental figure. Therapists support clients in doing inner child work and act as the parent figure until the individual works through their issues. As you go through this section of the book, I invite you to ask yourself, "How would a loving parent respond to me right now?" Often this is a helpful guide for you to understand how you can treat yourself lovingly, but also support yourself in doing hard things. A loving parent will support and encourage you to go to the dentist even if you are afraid and don't want to go.

Reparenting also includes how to be a mentally well, mature adult. Adulting 101 if you will. Why does this matter in the context of changing your relationship with alcohol? If you are reading this book, you have probably been using alcohol to cope with the daily stress of life in some capacity. Therefore, if you want to stop drinking or change your relationship with alcohol so that you are empowered in your decision and not "needing" a drink, it is vital that you learn the skills of reparenting. Otherwise, the next time you encounter stress, or any other situation or emotion you previously used alcohol to numb, you are going to want a drink (whether you are conscious that this is the reason or not).

Alcohol (as well as other unhealthy coping skills) has been known to stunt emotional maturity. In the case of Andrea, she drinks alcohol and tries to be perfect in order to feel like she's in control and avoid dealing with emotions and stress. As a result, she never learned how to self-soothe, process her emotions, or deal with the uncertainty that is simply a part of being human. In my experience of working with hundreds of women with alcohol use disorder, they all have one thing in common: They struggle to deal with unpredictability and difficulties of life. More than being addicted to alcohol, they are addicted to the *feeling* of being in control of their emotions and the ability to numb the emotions that they don't want to feel. The problem is, once you stop drinking (or start drinking less and more mindfully), you will no longer have the emotional lubricant to deal with life and will need to start facing difficult feelings head-on. This is why reparenting and building the life skills to create resiliency and take care of yourself are so important. It's a vital step in learning to thrive without depending on an escape route.

With my clients, I teach four tools of reparenting:

1. Mindfulness
2. Emotional Regulation
3. Self-Care
4. Boundaries

I will be dedicating an entire chapter to each of the tools in this section, so you can fully understand the importance of them and how to apply them to your life. But here's a quick overview.

The word "mindfulness" is defined as "the quality or state of being conscious or aware of something."[1] It allows us to notice our thoughts and then detach from them so we can engage in self-inquiry. Therefore, mindfulness is the first and most important tool because it creates a foundation, allowing us to understand our patterns, our motivation, and our unmet needs and build skills so we can act in a more conscious manner. We first need to be able to notice our patterns and recurring thoughts before we can start to honor and process our emotions.

Emotional regulation involves learning how to process and regulate your emotions. The goal of emotional regulation is not to "become less emotional" as some readers may think, but instead to learn how to thoughtfully identify how you feel, learn from the information your body is providing, and process it so that you are less likely to have your emotions bubble up at an inopportune time.

Self-care involves understanding and meeting your needs. Rather than bubble baths or facials, the type of self-care I will teach you involves balancing accountability with radical self-compassion so you can develop into your highest self. Self-compassion is a crucial part of this work so that you can learn how to grow and experiment without beating yourself up and falling into a shame spiral. Though you will never arrive in your self-care journey, you can learn how to continuously maintain your self-care regardless of what life throws at you.

Finally, boundaries will allow you to be in relationships with others in a way that feels both nourishing and respects your needs. It will free you from resentment and allow you to form true connections with others that are based on love, respect, and choice rather than obligation. Most of our parental figures tend to fall on one side of the spectrum or the other with boundaries. They either lack boundaries and are enmeshed with others or are closed off to connection, display issues with trust, and have walls to keep people out. Boundaries allow for healthy flexibility, so you retain your sense of self but also are able to depend on important people in your life whom you trust.

Most of us will benefit from learning all these skills, but we usually have one or two that will help us the most, depending on our history and patterns. The tools also tend to overlap and feed off each other. However, mindfulness is important to start with as it creates a foundation for the remaining three tools. Before working through our emotions, we must be able to notice the thought patterns that are intertwined with such emotions and that contribute to them.

For instance, Andrea's ability to cope with life would drastically improve if she learned how to regulate her emotions, engage in self-care, and set boundaries. When you think about your own upbringing and what you learned or didn't learn based on how your caregivers acted or talked about mindfulness, emotions, self-care, and boundaries, this will start to give you an idea of what learning and unlearning you may need to do.

In this section you will learn how your alcohol consumption is filling in the gaps of where you don't meet your needs to take care of yourself. Take a look back at the initial questionnaire you completed from Chapter 1. What were common areas or themes of your drinking habits? Are you mostly using alcohol to cope with your emotions and to relieve stress? You will need to work on emotional regulation. Do you rely on alcohol as your social lubricant when you are at social events, work happy hours, and dates? You likely need to prioritize self-care. Are you using it to cope with your relationship with your partner and family? You probably need to focus on boundaries. Looking at your questionnaire will give you a good idea of where you rely on alcohol to cope and where you need to focus when it comes to reparenting.

If you're still unsure if reparenting is for you, here are some common signs that you may benefit from reparenting. Some of these may seem like complete opposites at first. This is intentional. The goal of reparenting is to bring you back from opposite ends of the functioning spectrum (between overfunctioning and underfunctioning) to find a healthy place in the middle, where you can truly be responsible for identifying and meeting your needs.

Below is a list of potential reasons you may benefit from reparenting. This is not an exhaustive list, nor is it a diagnosis or an assessment of your caregivers' support for you. Be sure to check in with yourself as you go through this list. Stop and come back if you need to and try to answer honestly and thoughtfully. It is meant as a jumping-off point for you to explore how and why reparenting may benefit you.

You may benefit from reparenting if . . .

- You struggle to sit alone without distraction
- You've tried to meditate but feel worse after
- Your caregivers (parents) didn't model how to have healthy conflict and disagreement
- Your caregivers didn't model how to process emotions, what emotions are, and why they are important
- One or more parent was emotionally unavailable
- Your feelings were often invalidated when you were young
- You were expected to take care of your siblings or others
- You struggle to identify how you feel
- You grew up in a family of divorce or with an absent parent
- Your parents didn't model boundaries or how to set them
- You are often late
- You are afraid of conflict
- You identify as a people pleaser
- You feel burned out
- You avoid phone calls
- You avoid paying your bills
- You buy things you cannot afford to treat yourself
- You apologize for things you know aren't your fault
- Your caregivers "overparented" you or were "helicopter parents"
- You struggle to say no
- You struggle to apologize, and people say you are defensive
- You are known as the "strong one" in your family or friend group
- You often feel guilty and responsible for how other people feel
- You were raised in a family where keeping things "in the family" was important
- You tend to become passive aggressive when frustrated

- You experience road rage
- You feel guilty taking time for yourself
- You struggle with feeling shame
- You struggle with procrastination
- You have experienced some sort of trauma
- You have struggled with self-sabotage
- You struggle with imposter syndrome
- You feel like people don't really know you or understand you
- You feel like no matter what you do or accomplish, it's never enough
- You fear commitment

Chapter 7

The Voice in Your Head

The voice in my head is an asshole!

—Dan Harris

"I drank last week and I'm really feeling over this." Brianna sits down with a thud on my couch.

"Okay, walk me through it," I say.

"I don't know, the week was stressful . . . busy, per usual, and before I realized it, I was having three glasses of wine Wednesday, Thursday, and Friday."

"Did you want to drink before you took the first sip?" Brianna had just abstained from alcohol for sixty days before last week. This setback surprises me a bit since she seemed to be doing really well.

"I don't know . . . I assume so since I drank," Brianna says nonchalantly.

"Okay, so you don't really remember having a craving?" I ask.

"Not really."

"Do you remember thinking anything to try to stop yourself from drinking?"

"No." Brianna stares at me blankly.

"Okay, do you remember what you said to yourself after you drank?"

"Said to myself . . . what do you mean?" I can tell Brianna is confused.

"You know . . . do you remember any specific thoughts you had before or after you drank last week?" I ask, hoping this rephrase will help her understand me. She still is staring at me blankly. So, I add, "Okay right now in this moment, what are you thinking? Or what is the voice in your head saying?"

"What do you mean 'the voice in my head?' Amanda, do you think I'm crazy or something?" Brianna says half teasing.

"I do not think you are crazy, Brianna. I don't think you actually have a voice. I'm talking about your inner voice, the part of you that is always thinking." I search Brianna's face for her recognition of what I am talking about. She doesn't seem to be getting it, so I say, "Shh, let's be quiet for a moment. It's easier to notice when we're not talking."

We pause for a minute. Brianna still stares at me blankly.

I add, "The voice is probably saying . . . what voice is she talking about?" I pause again, "Or this seems longer than a minute." I pause again. "Or . . . this really feels like a waste of time."

A smile slowly spreads across her face. "Okay, now I get it."

I smile. "Great. We all have a voice in our heads that sounds like us. Some people call it an 'inner roommate' or 'monkey mind.' It's the part of you that is always thinking."

"Okay . . . yeah I just have never really thought of that before."

"A lot of us haven't. But one of the most important things we can do as we start to heal our relationship with alcohol and reparent ourselves is learn to practice mindfulness."

"You mean like sitting cross-legged?"

I laugh. "I'm glad you said that actually because that is a big misconception of mindfulness. Mindfulness is not meditation. Mindfulness is the state of being aware and noticing the present moment, which includes paying attention to your thoughts and emotions. Just as there is a voice in your head that is always thinking, there is also a part of you that is listening to the thinking."

"Right, that makes sense."

"So, when we can start to get better at separating our thinking self from our observing self, the more we will be able to actually notice what we are thinking about in the moment. And that is where the power lies because we then have more control over which thoughts we pay attention to and take seriously."

"But with all due respect, Amanda, why does this matter? I want to stop drinking, not become a yoga teacher."

I smile. "That's a really good question. The truth is that mindfulness is actually one of the most important tools to help us stop drinking. Right now, you struggle to identify what thoughts lead you to drink, so if you start to be more mindful and notice what thoughts you have as you go to open the wine bottle, pour the glass, how you convince yourself that you will just have one . . . this will give you the power to slow down and interrupt that train of thought and do something else instead."

"Okay, that makes sense. How do I start?"

Mindfulness

Unless you have practiced yoga, meditation, or mindfulness, you may not be familiar with the fact that our "mind" is actually composed of two distinct parts: the part of you that is narrating the world around you and actively thinking (also known as the voice in your head), and the part of you that is listening to that voice. We all have both of these parts, though it is common to overly identify with the part of us that is actively thinking. When those two distinct parts of our mind get blurred and stuck together, it is difficult to differentiate between our thoughts, emotions, and reactions. Instead, everything feels like it's happening at once and we may feel like we don't have control over our response to stimuli. Mindfulness is the first step in breaking out of this and getting our power back because it allows us to notice our physiological body responses, thoughts, and emotions. It's important because if we cannot identify the part of ourselves that observes things, we have no ability to be self-aware. Mindfulness is a powerful tool that allows us to notice our patterns so we can break them and choose behavior that is in alignment with our values.

When we are not aware of our thoughts or internal dialogue, we may believe we *are* our thoughts. We *have* thoughts, but we are not our thoughts. When we don't understand this crucial difference, we can get "stuck" in our thoughts. This is also known as cognitive fusion. Have you ever watched a movie and identified so much with the main character's struggle that you forgot the movie wasn't real? Maybe your body even responded by feeling queasy or your heart raced while watching because you got so absorbed in the plot. This is similar to being stuck in our thoughts. When we are in a state of cognitive fusion, we are more likely to believe that our thoughts are truth. This can cause a lot of pain and suffering.

If we believe all our thoughts are true, then we will likely believe that we are a bad friend when we think *Shut up!* when a friend is talking, and we are annoyed. We think we are a bad mom if we have the thought *I just want to get away from my kids for a little bit!* Or we may think we don't love our spouse or there is something wrong with our relationship if we have the thought *That guy is so attractive.* We shame ourselves for thinking this because we believe that we are our thoughts. However, the truth is all human beings have random and intrusive thoughts and they have no actual bearing on who we are as a person or our values. Those of us with mental health issues such as anxiety, depression, and Obsessive-Compulsive Disorder (OCD) are also much more prone to cognitive fusion than the average person, so this is especially important to know.

Cognitive fusion can make us spend a lot of time and energy trying to fight our thoughts and get them to go away. When we are in this state, our thoughts feel urgent . . . like a blinking light in your car indicating that you are out of windshield wiper fluid. While this blinking light doesn't make a huge difference while you are driving right now (especially compared to your gas gauge), the blinking, like our thoughts, feels urgent, intrusive, and important to get done NOW! Cognitive fusion can even make our thoughts that are about the past or the future feel like they are happening in the present moment.* Therefore, it makes sense that most times our reaction to being stuck in our thoughts is to try to fight them and wrestle them into going away. Maybe this example will sound familiar. . . .

Your phone alarm blares in your ear as you fling your eyes open. It's a Monday morning at 6 a.m. Your first thought is *So tired!* You didn't sleep well last night. You grab your phone clumsily as you attempt to silence the blaring sound and reset the alarm for another fifteen minutes. Then you remember you set a goal to start getting up earlier. You say to yourself, "Remember the goal! You said you wanted to get up earlier to practice gratitude in the morning."

The (same) voice responds to itself saying, "Not today, I will start tomorrow."

"No, you've said that before, get up! You aren't going to do it tomorrow!"

"Yes! I will! Just let me sleep!"

---

* Cognitive fusion is a completely distinct state from a flashback that is associated with trauma and/or PTSD.

"You are so pathetic!"

This is often referred to as the devil and angel on your shoulder, but the truth is the voice is the same. Both are parts of your thinking mind. You aren't the devil or the angel; you are the one who is listening to them both. But what cartoons get wrong about this example is that rather than listening to these characters and weighing out the options, you have a right to not fight with either. Fighting with your negative thoughts makes them stronger. Similar to a Chinese finger trap, the harder we try to make our anxious thoughts go away, the stronger these thoughts become, and we end up getting even more stuck in our thoughts.

How do we escape this cycle? We practice mindfulness. We can notice the thoughts that we are having and remember that we are not *them*. We *accept* that we have these unpleasant thoughts or feelings and, instead of fighting them, allow them to be there. We make room for them, just as when you relax your fingers in the finger trap, only then is the space created to move them out. The next time you find yourself fighting with your anxious, depressed, or unhelpful thoughts, try to take them less seriously. You can say, "Thanks for sharing" and take action based on your values. Contrary to popular belief, you do not have to agree with your thoughts or the devil or angel on your shoulder in order to take an action. You don't have to listen to either one's argument and can instead practice mindfulness and take the best action to take care of yourself based on what you need. We can practice acceptance and recognize that while we may never "get rid of" our negative thoughts, we can learn to live with them, and this lessens their power. Acceptance does not mean that we like our thoughts. It does not mean that we approve of them or are happy about their presence. It does mean that we stop fighting with them and instead start focusing our time and energy on how we can take care of ourselves.

If you are struggling to see why this small shift makes a difference, consider the importance of your acceptance if you have ever struggled to fall asleep. Imagine, you are in your room, tossing and turning and struggling to sleep. You need to sleep because you have a big presentation at work tomorrow. But the more you stare at the clock, the more you calculate how many potential hours of sleep you will get, and thus the more restless and frustrated you grow. This of course only makes you more alert. Only when you stop getting angry at yourself for not being able to fall asleep and practice acceptance, can you do something calming, like take a bath or read a book, and try falling asleep again. The same is true of your thoughts. Remember, as we talked about in Chapter 2, your brain is essentially a "don't get killed device."[1] It evolved to keep you alive at all costs. Your brain cannot tell the difference between the stress from your work meeting tomorrow and the threat of a lion about to eat you. So, of course, it is a natural response for your brain to feel extra alert the night before an important presentation. Try to remember this the next time you are experiencing obtrusive or unhelpful thoughts.

Ways to Defuse Your Thoughts

Practice a grounding skill to get you into the present moment:
- Example: 5-4-3-2-1
- List 5 things you can see
  - ▷ 4 things you can touch
  - ▷ 3 things you can hear
  - ▷ 2 things you can smell
  - ▷ 1 thing you can taste

- Get out of your head by becoming present in your body:
  - ▷ Engage your senses

    Smell: smell an essential oil, light a candle, bake some cookies

    Touch: play with putty, rub an ice cube on your hands, splash cold water on your face, feel the texture of different pillows or textiles

    Taste: suck on a mint, drink tea, brush your teeth

    Hearing: listen to music, the sound of a crackling fire, or ASMR (autonomous sensory meridian response, which you can find online)

    Sight: look at a painting or watch a candle flicker
  - ▷ Do something that promotes sensation in your body: get a massage or massage yourself, practice gua sha, take a hot bath or shower, stretch, exercise, exfoliate your skin, engage in myofascial release, masturbate
- Rather than saying "I think or feel __," practice saying "I am having the thought that __." This allows us to subtly remind ourselves that we are distinct from our thoughts and having a thought doesn't mean you have to listen to it.
- Imagine your distressing thoughts as words that are on a movie screen. Picture yourself in the theater watching your thoughts in front of you. See the distance between yourself and your thoughts and remind yourself that you have the ability to watch your thoughts and not listen to them.
- Imagine your thoughts coming from a person sitting next to you. If this person told you to do something, you would not automatically take their words seriously. Practice examining your own thoughts as though they are not yours.

- We can sometimes get caught up in whether our thoughts are true or not. Instead practice asking yourself, "Is this thought helpful?" If it is not supporting you in moving toward your values and living the life you want, it is not a helpful thought and you do not need to listen to it.

Practicing Mindfulness IRL

"I don't think the mindfulness stuff we talked about last week is working," Brianna tells me at the beginning of her next session.

"Okay, walk me through it," I say.

"So, I have been trying to notice my thoughts and feelings more, like we talked about. I realize stress is definitely a trigger for me to drink. Not like during the middle of it, but like after I put the kids to bed and sit on the couch. Especially when my husband isn't home yet; he's been working a lot of night shifts at the hospital . . . oh I didn't even realize it, that's a trigger too."

"Good," I say.

"Yeah, like I'm noticing more things like we talked about. But it didn't help! I still drank. On Tuesday I was cleaning the kitchen and I started looking at a wine bottle. I noticed myself looking at it and I tried to pause like we talked about and take a few deep breaths. I counted to thirty and tried to keep cleaning the kitchen but the feeling didn't go away. So, I drank."

"This is good information though, Brianna. I want to be clear; mindfulness isn't a solution to not drinking. Being mindful of wanting to drink or noticing you have a craving won't make it go away. Even pausing or practicing mindfulness skills won't just eradicate it. But this does help with us starting to understand your triggers more, which *will* help you in the future."

"Okay." Brianna sighs, disappointed.

"Let me ask, when you noticed you wanted to drink, why didn't you get out of the kitchen and try to go into another room so you wouldn't see the wine bottles?" I ask. I have already tried to talk to Brianna about not keeping alcohol in her home, but they have a large wine collection and Brianna is adamant about being able to keep the bottles there for her husband and when guests come over.

"Because after counting to thirty, I still wanted to drink. I was so mad at myself. Like why do I keep doing this to myself? I just started drinking."

"Got it. Okay, so this is really important, Brianna. It's important to also normalize that you are going to have cravings and thoughts about drinking. You are still in the habit of drinking. Of course, you are going to want to drink, especially if you are stressed and your husband isn't home. The more you accept that you are going to have these intrusive thoughts, rather than getting mad about them, the easier it will be to not listen to them. The angrier you get at your thoughts or the more you try to suppress them, the stronger they get. You also are not thinking these thoughts about drinking on purpose. Try to practice some compassion for yourself that this is hard."

"Okay, so what should I do when I notice the urge to drink, besides, I know, leave the room?"

"One really powerful mindfulness skill that you can use in the present moment is called RAIN." I stand up and drawn R-A-I-N on my chalkboard. Under each letter I write, Recognize, Allow, Investigate, and Nonattachment. "When a thought comes up like a *glass of wine would be so nice right now*, practice noticing the thought you are having and allow it to come up. Then try to get curious about why you may be thinking this. For example, asking yourself, 'what emotion am I feeling right now?' and 'is there a better way I could manage my stress?' You are going to want to start noticing what may be contributing to these thoughts."

"Okay and what about nonattachment? What is that?"

"Nonattachment essentially means you try not to attach to your thoughts. You recognize that you don't have control over your automatic thoughts. You aren't thinking them on purpose. It makes sense that you are going to want to drink when you are stressed right now because your brain is in the habit of doing that to deal with stress lately."

"Okay, I will try that for next week."

"Keep practicing mindfulness, Brianna. It will get easier with practice. Here is a list of different ways to practice mindfulness beyond just counting and breathing."

While it may be tempting to rush through or not practice the list below, nonattachment and mindfulness is the backbone of reparenting. When you are stuck in your thoughts and unable to distinguish yourself from them, it will be extremely difficult to be able to identify and process your emotions (the next chapter), take care of yourself (Chapter 9) and teach others how to treat you (Chapter 10).

Ways to Practice Mindfulness

- While taking a bath or shower, smell your soap, notice the temperature of the water, feel the texture of your loofah, massage your scalp as you shampoo.
- While eating, slow down and notice the texture and taste of your food. Chew slowly and notice how the texture of the food changes as it starts to break down. Notice how your stomach fullness changes as you eat.
- While brushing your teeth, taste the toothpaste, feel the suds in your mouth, notice the texture of the bristles on your teeth.

- While doing a chore or cleaning (examples: washing dishes, vacuuming, mopping, making a bed), notice the physical sensations. For example, if you are washing dishes, notice the smell of the soap, the feeling and temperature of the water on your skin, how hard you have to scrub to get the plate clean.
- Do a mindful breathing exercise. Try breathing in for a count of four, holding for four, and exhaling to a count of four. Butterfly tapping is another great technique. Cross your arms and put one hand on each shoulder. Tap each hand individually on your shoulder while taking deep breaths. The tapping on both sides of your body, known as bilateral stimulation, will calm your parasympathetic nervous system.
- Do a body scan (notice the sensations in your body).
- Practice yoga or another form of movement where you can slow down and notice the sensations in your body without distraction.
- Go on a mindful walk or hike, noticing nature as you move.
- Listen to music.
- Do a puzzle.
- Use a coloring book.
- Meditate (use an app or guided meditation, notice your breath, notice your heartbeat, do a body scan).

Chapter 8

Emotions 101

**Feelings are like children. You don't want them driving the
car, but you don't want to stuff them in the trunk either.**
—Thanks for Sharing (2013)

"God, I remember why I drink!" Tara says as we begin our session for
the week.

"Why is that?" I ask.

"Because I hate myself, I hate this, I hate everyone!" She says it in
an exaggerated way as if she is joking, but I know Tara well enough to
know that there is definitely truth in that statement.

"Tell me what's going on?"

"Oh, ya know, I just really want to drink because everything is
terrible."

"Did something happen?" I ask.

"I mean not really, but I just was accused of stealing my coworker's
purse at work. And I didn't. . . ." Tara looks down at the floor as she
thinks. "You know what, I don't need this. Not if people are going to
be petty and shit. I think I'm just going to quit."

"That really sucks, Tara," I say honestly.

Tara becomes uncomfortable with my honest response and her guard soars back up. "Oh well, I can get another job. It's just waitressing. Not like I have a resume to worry about," she says.

"Yes, you could do that. But before we talk about your plans, I'm wondering, how are you feeling?"

"Fine."

"Well, a few minutes ago you said that everything was terrible. That doesn't seem fine to me . . ." I say carefully.

"I don't know. I never know how to answer that question, Amanda. I don't know how I feel."

"Good."

"What do you mean good?"

"I've been seeing you for months and this is the first time you've recognized you don't know how you feel. This is progress. In the past, you've always insisted you're fine or not been able to honestly talk about your emotions. Recognizing you don't know how you feel is an important place to start."

"All right, all right, you caught me."

"It's also pretty amazing that you didn't drink after this happened."

"Well, it happened this morning. I was thinking about drinking. I almost didn't show up for my appointment."

I smile. "I appreciate the honesty." And I really do. The fact that Tara came to her appointment today after what happened at work is really good progress. We've been in a cycle for a few months now where Tara stops drinking for about a month, then something happens, she gets upset, skips her appointment, and drinks. We've talked about how her emotions are connected with her drinking and she seems to know this logically but has not yet been able to recognize that she doesn't actually know how she feels.

"You coming to your appointment today gives us the time to pause and actually put into practice some of the coping skills we've talked about rather than your pattern of just reacting and drinking whenever something doesn't go your way."

"Okay, I paused, now what do I do?" Tara asks.

I smile. "So quick to rush the solution, aren't we? And by we, I mean as human beings we all have this tendency."

"Okay . . . so I just do nothing?"

"Well, typically if a stressor comes into our life or we experience something frustrating, pausing rather than reacting is generally a good idea. Not to be cliché, but I really recommend taking a breath to create a moment of intentional mindfulness." I take a deep breath, and Tara does the same.

"Good. Okay, Tara, so I want you to get curious and notice, how does your body feel? What sensations are you experiencing right now?"

"What do you mean?"

"Well, our emotions are not always obvious to us, but they all typically have some kind of physical body sensation that accompanies them. Different emotions can feel differently in everyone. For example, when I feel shame, my stomach drops, and I tend to feel nauseous. When I feel anxious, my heart tends to beat faster, my hands get shaky. So, when you are trying to notice how you feel, the first thing to do is to take a body scan. Are you open to doing one with me?"

"Honestly every part of me wants to make fun of this right now."

"I know," I say. "Let's try it. Try to step out of the skepticism."

Tara's skepticism reminds me a bit of my own when I landed myself in therapy because of my drinking. I had no interest in identifying how I

felt because I didn't care how I felt or why I felt that way. I just wanted
to FEEL BETTER! Maybe you relate to this too. The truth is, neither
I nor anyone else can make you feel better or make your emotions go
away. However, I do have some techniques to help you better identify,
understand, and process your emotions, so you can experience greater
emotional regulation (which does make your emotions easier to deal
with and over time can make you feel better).

According to Marc Brackett, PhD, the founder and director of the
Yale Center for Emotional Intelligence, three out of four individuals
are not able to identify how they feel.[1] This statistic matters because
the better we are able to identify (starting with our body sensations)
and label our emotions, the better we are able to regulate and cope
with our emotions. If you are reading this book, it's likely that you too
may struggle to identify how you feel. That is what this chapter is all
about. We are going to explore practical tools so you can learn to identify how you feel and cope with your emotions in a productive way.
Then you can make conscious choices rather than defaulting to your
automatic reactions.

This work is also crucial because most of us who are drinking too
much are using alcohol to cope with and regulate our emotions. You
may not even recognize you are doing this. Like Tara, you just know
that something happens, you experience a life stressor, and boom!—
you're pouring yourself another glass of wine. We are building off the
previous chapter of mindfulness by using that skill to turn inward
and identify not just your thought patterns but your body sensations.
Learning how to identify and regulate your emotions does not mean
that you suppress your emotions or become a robot who doesn't feel
anything. The goal of emotional regulation is to empower you to be
able to identify your emotions so you can process them, get your needs
met, and make decisions out of choice rather than as a reaction to your

emotions. If we are stuck in the habit of doing things that have negative consequences in order to deal with our emotions, it is going to be difficult to create a fulfilling and purposeful life.

The Evolution of Emotions

Our brains evolved in order to regulate our bodies. As our bodies evolved and got more complex, our brain grew in order to be able to keep all our different body functions running properly. The ability of our brains to consciously notice the changes that are happening in our body is known as interoception. Interoception is the awareness of your physical body sensations, including heart rate, breathing, digestion, pain, and many more that we aren't even consciously aware of. These sensations also inform us about what is going on in our body so we can take action in order to meet our needs. Of course, we are not able to feel *everything* that is going on in our body. That would be too much information for us to handle. There are many biological processes that happen in our body without our awareness or control, such as the blood moving through your body or your immune system fighting off a pathogen.

We only are aware of things that are necessary for us to notice so we can take action. According to emotion researcher Lisa Feldman Barrett, your brain is continuously monitoring its "body budget." You notice if you have enough food, water, sleep, safety, etc., making predictions about how long you will be able to sustain yourself at your current levels and prompting you to take action in order to regulate it and achieve allostasis.[2] Remember, allostasis is the process of getting your body back into homeostasis after a stressor or stimuli.

Emotions are an outgrowth of the process of regulating your body budget. They start with physiological changes in your body. But these sensations do not necessarily make sense until you add in context about what your current sensation is. For example, you would interpret a stomachache very differently depending on whether you just ate something (you ate too much or something you ate didn't agree with you), haven't eaten (you're hungry), or you're satisfied with your meal. In the case of the latter, it may make you think your stomachache is less about your stomach and more about your mental state. You may wonder if you are worried or anxious instead. This is known as categorization. Without context, it is difficult to identify your emotions because contrary to pop psychology, research has debunked the idea that there are hardwired "core emotions" built into us that are universally experienced. Instead, Barrett discusses in her groundbreaking research how emotions are *constructed* based on your physiological body changes, your brain trying to predict what is going to happen next (based on your past experiences), and the context of your current situation, which allows you to take relevant action.[3]

This does not mean that emotions are not *real*. However, the ability to use language is a requirement for emotions to exist because emotions are created through words. This is why infants and other mammals do not experience emotions in our traditional sense of the word. Instead, they can feel high or low pleasantness and high or low energy, which makes up the basis for how our emotions are constructed. However, adult brains are so quick to put together context clues that according to Barrett, "emotions seem to be 'happening to' you, when in fact your brain is actively constructing the experience, held in check by the state of the world and your body."

We also learn about the concept of emotions from our environment and culture. Adults in our life teach us what emotions "look like" and these lessons are reinforced by the media. We learn that being sad looks like frowning and being angry looks like furrowing your eyebrows. But we don't learn about what an emotion may feel like internally. The truth is the physical expression of emotions looks very different depending on the person, and emotions can also be experienced and felt differently. This is important to know so that you can effectively regulate your emotions, which is crucial if you want to stop drinking.

How to Process Your Emotions

As a therapist, I have learned a lot about emotions over the years and there are different ways to teach people how to regulate them based on the therapeutic modality you study. Therapists often encourage people to "process" their emotions, but most people do not know how to do that or what that actually looks like. I created an acronym to teach you how to process or work through your emotions step-by-step. When we get into the habit of processing and tending to our emotions as they come up, we improve our ability to regulate our emotions and effectively take care of ourselves. NAILER stands for **Notice, Allow, Investigate, Label, Explore**, and **Release**. Start by **noticing** the physical sensations in your body and how you feel, **allow** them to come up rather than resisting the feeling, **investigate** what is going on, get curious about what emotion you may be feeling, **label** it, **explore** what things you could do in order to work through that emotion, and take action to **release** it. Let's break down each of these steps.

Notice

The first part of processing your emotions involves noticing what you are feeling. As we discussed, emotions start in our bodies as a physiological sensation. This is the first step in an emotion being created. If you are someone who struggles to identify your physiological sensations or how your body feels, remember that it takes practice to improve your interoception. If we are not in the habit of practicing mindfulness or noticing how we are feeling emotionally or physically, it can be easy for us to miss these first cues of an emotion. Slowing down and practicing mindfulness like we talked about in the last chapter is a good place to start.

Let's practice right now. First, read through the instructions below to get a sense of the exercise. Then pause; I recommend getting still in order to really focus and notice the sensations that are going on in your body. Close your eyes and do this body scan.

Start at the top of your head. Notice your scalp. Is there any tightness or itchiness there? What about your forehead . . . any tension?

What about your eyes . . . are they heavy, itchy, stinging?

What about your cheeks . . . are you feeling flushed or hot at all?

How about your jaw . . . is it tight? Wiggle it around for a moment and notice how that feels. What about your throat . . . is it feeling tight at all? How does it feel when you take a deep breath?

What about your shoulders . . . are they tight? Are they feeling up by your ears? Is there any neck or shoulder pain? What about your chest? Does that change when you take a breath? Is your heart rate feeling elevated at all? Are your hands clammy?

What about your stomach? Can you notice the sensations of hunger, fullness, or satiety? Do you feel any pain or nausea? Do you have any soreness or achiness in your body?

Are your legs restless?

Sometimes taking small movements or wiggles during this process can help you notice any sensation that you were not aware of initially. You could also practice this by doing some jumping jacks to get your heart rate up and then take a break and notice how it calms down to normal, feeling the different temperature changes in your body.

This exercise is not meant to make you feel an emotion that you were not already experiencing. When we do a body scan, not all information is relevant to your emotional state. You may feel soreness in your legs because you went for a run yesterday or feel full because you just had lunch. The point of this exercise is to improve your interoception . . . to get you familiar and more skilled at noticing all the input and sensations in your body so that you can more accurately identify your emotions. As you get more skilled at it, you will begin to understand your own emotional patterns, or how emotions feel to you. For example, some people feel nervousness through a tight chest, while others may tend to be prone to stomachaches. This is not to say your emotions will always feel *exactly* the same way. However, most of us do fall into typical patterns of how we experience our emotions.

Ways to Increase Interoception

- Practice mindfulness and all the skills I listed on pages 97–98 in the previous chapter.
- Practice meditation.
- Get a massage, acupuncture, or other body work.
- Engage in self-massage or self-touch.
- Engage in movement that has a mindfulness component to it, like yoga.
- Practice eating mindfully and notice the sensations of hunger, fullness, and satiation.
- Stretch your body and notice the sensations of how different movements feel in your body.

Allow

One of the biggest barriers that prevents us from processing our emotions is that we do not want to feel them. The sensation is uncomfortable, and we try to ignore or numb our emotions by drinking or doing any other of a host of activities. We may not even realize we are doing this. If you are someone who identifies as not being very "emotional" or feels as though you really do not experience many emotions, you may be in such a habit of distracting yourself, numbing, or checking out that you do it automatically. There's nothing wrong with distraction. It serves a very useful purpose for us. We cannot always stop in the middle of a meeting and feel our feelings and work through them. Distracting ourselves until we can be present with our emotions is an important technique. If emotions also get very overwhelming for us, it can be helpful to distract ourselves and take a break for a bit. The problem is when we chronically check out and continuously avoid feeling our feelings. As Marc Brackett says, "If we don't express our emotions, they pile up like debt that will eventually come due."[4] Take your time with it; it is going to take practice to slow down and start noticing your body sensations.

Another thing that prevents us from processing our emotions is judging ourselves. It looks something like this. Maybe we start to recognize based on our body sensations that we may be feeling blue. We do not want to feel this way so immediately we start to judge ourselves. Rather than allowing ourselves to feel the way we do we start having thoughts like *What's wrong with me? I shouldn't be feeling sad right now. Other people have it way worse than me. I'm so pathetic.* If noticing your emotions leads to judgment, you are not actually allowing yourself to feel your emotions. It is a way that we check out of our current emotion and try to regain control. For many of us, it can feel

Emotions

A biological state brought on by neuropsychological changes associated with thoughts, mood, and a degree of pleasure or displeasure.

Example: sadness

Meta-Emotions

An emotion you have about your emotions that prevents you from working through how you actually feel, and/or a judgment about your emotions that evokes an emotional response.

Example: being angry about feeling sad

better to beat ourselves up or judge ourselves rather than surrender to an emotion that we do not have direct control over.

Ironically, the judgment of our emotions often leads us to experience something called a meta-emotion. Meta-emotions are emotions *about* your emotions. Instead of being curious about why we may be feeling how we are feeling, we stay stuck in thinking about why we shouldn't feel this way. Most commonly, I tend to see people feel anger or shame about feeling sad or about an emotion someone perceives as "weak." However, you can easily have any combination of emotions. You can feel sad about being sad or angry about feeling sad or angry about feeling angry. You can also feel more than one emotion at the same time.

Investigate

Context matters, especially when it comes to understanding our emotions. While emotions start in the body with physiological changes, they become more specific and complex when we add in the context of our life and social norms. Understanding what happened right before we felt emotional gives us important clues to understand what emotion we may be feeling and how we can take action to work through it. Questions like "Why may I be feeling this way?" can help us understand and make sense of our physiological sensations and the thoughts that follow. This is also an important question for us to understand when we are exploring our relationship with alcohol or another addictive behavior. Realizing why you may be feeling a certain way can help you get your needs met in a different way rather than picking up a drink. However, questions like "What is wrong with me?" lead us to feel shame and guilt, both of which are laden with judgment. Instead, be compassionate toward yourself. Ask yourself questions in the same way you would ask a friend or a child. I use the word "investigate" because I want you to examine and research your body and emotions, like a scientist.

Leaning into curiosity instead of judgment is one of the most effective ways to investigate your emotions and gain more understanding into why you may be feeling the way that you are. This is not always easy. As Brackett says, "There may be a complex web of events and memories, of one emotion provoking another. Usually, asking one question will lead to more questions, a succession of follow-ups that can go deep."[5] Oftentimes as you start to investigate your emotional experience, the intensity of your emotions may increase. This is okay and to be expected. This does not mean it will last forever. The sensations of emotions are experienced in waves, with peaks of intensity that will soon recede if you can be with them rather than running from them.

Questions to Ask Yourself:

- Why may I be feeling this way?
- Why now?

- What just happened? What may be triggering this emotion?
- What was I doing before this happened? Or this morning or last night?
- Do I have memories connected to this experience, person, or situation?
- Have I met my basic needs? Am I hungry, thirsty, lonely, tired? Have I been outside today?

Questions to Avoid:

- What is wrong with me?
- Why do I always feel this way?
- Why can't I make this feeling go away?
- Why can't I figure this out?
- Why can't I just be happy?

Label

The goal of investigating is to support you in being able to accurately label how you feel. If you did the body scan and are still struggling to identify how you may be feeling right now, a helpful place to start is by recognizing if you are feeling high or low energy and high or low pleasantness. These two spectrums are hardwired into your brain, and unlike emotions, they are felt even by infants. Babies may not be able to have the concept of hunger or boredom, but they do know and communicate their energy level and pleasantness.[6] If you feel slightly high energy and slightly low pleasantness, you feel peeved. If you feel slightly low energy and slightly low pleasantness, you feel apathetic. If you feel slightly low energy and slightly high pleasantness, you feel at ease. With slightly high energy and slightly high pleasantness, you feel pleasant. This is known as the circumplex model of affect.[7] As you go up the scale of intensity of both pleasantness and energy, the more intense the emotion becomes. My favorite chart to help you easily identify your emotions is created by Marc Brackett and known as the mood meter. I recommend searching for it online, or he has a free app you can download to help you identify exactly what emotion you feel.

It may seem unimportant to find the *exact* word that describes how you are feeling, but research shows that there is a direct correlation between the number of emotion words someone knows and the prevalence of mood disorders. The higher someone's emotional vocabulary, known as emotional granularity,[8] the better they are able to regulate their emotions. That is, the more specifically you can identify the exact emotions you are feeling, and understand the distinct differences between different emotion words, the better you are able to understand how you feel and take action that supports you. Having high emotional granularity also saves your brain time and energy. You can hear your alarm clock go off in the morning, experience the sensation of tiredness, and immediately feel depressed (if you dislike your job for example). The same person who is starting a new job that day could feel immediately nervous and alert. The better your emotional vocabulary, the less time you will need to spend investigating how and why you feel the way you do.

Children in general have a much smaller emotional vocabulary than adults, and as a result, they tend to feel emotions more intensely and unpredictably. When we cannot adequately understand why we are feeling a certain way or what variables may be influencing our mood and emotions, it is much more difficult for us to make changes or take actions to help us feel better. Most children only have three words to describe how they feel: happy, sad, and mad. If those are the only three words you have to describe how you are feeling, you are going to feel one of those emotions about one third of your life. However, if a child starts to identify the difference between feeling frustrated instead of angry, for example, this will reduce the intensity of the emotion they feel and allow them to better process and regulate their emotions.

I highly recommend looking up definitions of different emotion words so you can learn the exact, precise word to use. Since there is no emotional education in our schools, many adults are not aware of differences between jealousy and envy or stress and pressure. The accuracy and specificity matter because being able to make sense of our body's sensations and the context of our environment helps us meet our goals and regulate our body budget. The words you know shape your experience of yourself, your body sensations, and the external stimuli around you. Have you ever heard that the Inuit and Yupik have dozens of words for snow?[9] Snow is such an important part of their lives that having many different words to precisely describe the exact kind of snow matters. This changes their understanding of snow. While you and I may just see regular snow, they have different words to communicate the differences between "fresh snow," "fine snow," and "soft deep snow." Similarly, other languages have different words for emotions. Learning new words for emotions is another great way to expand your emotional vocabulary. For example, there is a German word, *schadenfreude*, which directly translates as "harm-joy" or the pleasure of watching someone fail or suffer. While you may be able to understand how you have potentially felt that way in the past, before you learned that word, you didn't have a full understanding of it. The word creates the experience of that emotion. And if you can precisely identify feeling that way, you have the capacity to understand yourself and others better.

Explore and Release

The final step of processing your emotions is to explore and release the sensations associated with them. The exploration part of this step involves asking yourself, what can I do to take care of myself right now? What do I need right now? The release involves taking direct action to regulate your body budget and bring yourself back to a place of homeostasis. If you have ever felt better emotionally after venting to a friend, going for a run, or screaming to a song in your car, this is because through those actions you were able to discharge some of the energy associated with that emotion and regulate your body budget. Remember, our bodies and brains are inextricably connected. Your body responds to stress by sending a cascade of hormones through your bloodstream to get ready for fight, flight, or freeze. Therefore, just because you notice your heart rate increasing, allow the sensations to wash over you, investigate why you may feel this way, and identify it as fear, doesn't mean that all those physiological body changes and hormones magically go away.

This is why the release is so important. In order to achieve allostasis, your body needs to know that it is safe. Humans also have an innate desire to understand what is happening to us and why so we can make predictions and keep ourselves safe in the future. Sometimes our emotions make perfect sense, and we are given a sense of closure. Sometimes we can identify the emotion we feel, but it still doesn't make sense to us, especially if we have trauma. If you allow yourself to feel your emotions and take action to release the emotions, you are regulating your emotions, regardless if you understand how this is happening. And if you are able to regulate your emotions, you are going to be able to better take care of yourself, both of which are huge components of reparenting.

Ways to Release Your Emotions and
Regulate Your Body Budget

- Move your body in some way (yoga, stretching, walking, running, jumping jacks, shaking, dancing, yelling, punching a pillow) . . . any type of movement lets your body budget get more regulated by sending signals to your brain that you are safe. Use slower movement if you are feeling high energy and want to decrease your heart rate; use higher energy/aerobic movement if you are feeling low energy. You can also play with temperatures. Cold sensations tend to increase your energy, while warmer temperatures will bring you down.

- Deep and slow breathing. Try inhaling for four counts, holding for four counts, and exhaling for four counts.

- Connect with others. Other people, even if we don't know them, can help us regulate our body budgets through coregulation. This can be as simple as smiling when you see a stranger or engaging in small talk, which reassures your brain that it is okay to get out of your head and be present in the world around you.

- Spend time with close friends or family. Spending time with people we love and trust is a very effective method of regulating our body budget. Studies show that if we are especially close to someone, we can sync up heart rates and breathing patterns while around each other. We're also more likely to engage in affection and touch—whether this is a kiss, a friendly pat on the back, or a platonic hug—and to laugh authentically when we are around loved ones, which also does wonders for reminding our brains that we are safe,[10] thus regulating our body budgets.

- Journal or share with someone what you are thinking and feeling.

- Do something creative that will allow you to express your emotions through it (painting, drawing, dancing, listening to music, singing, playing an instrument, etc.).
- Cry. Scientists have recently discovered that we have different types of tears. Tears that we get when cutting an onion (basal tears) have a different composition than emotional tears (psychic tears), which have neurotransmitters that are released during times of stress.[11] Thus, allowing yourself to cry helps regulate your body budget by purging stress chemicals.

Chapter 9

Self-Care

Self-care feels different when it is a
love letter rather than a saving grace.

—Ilyse Kennedy

"I think it may be a good time to talk about self-care," I say to Andrea.

"I feel like I have really good self-care. I exercise almost every day."

I smile. "Maybe I should start by asking, what does the word 'self-care' mean to you?"

"I mean I know Instagram acts like it's bath bombs, but I know that it is more about habits. Exercising daily. Making sure to eat healthy and limit sugar. Not procrastinating because that's not taking care of yourself. It's about being the best version of yourself," Andrea says proudly.

"Yes, a lot of that *can* be self-care. But self-care is actually a highly specific, ever-changing practice of meeting your needs. So, self-care is going to look different from week to week or month to month."

"Yeah, I mean mine does change but I don't really want it too. I feel like I'm either following through with all my self-care or not doing it."

"What does *not* doing self-care look like to you?" I ask.

"Sleeping in, not exercising, eating like crap."

"What if that actually is self-care?"

Andrea is surprised. "What do you mean? That's the opposite of self-care."

"Maybe. But perhaps when you are falling out of your self-care routine, your body and mind are actually really needing a break. Maybe this is a way you are meeting your needs."

"I guess. I just feel like if it was self-care, it would feel better. I wouldn't feel bad about myself afterwards."

"Well, I think it is hard to feel good about taking a break, resting, or sleeping in when you believe you should never break your routine," I offer.

"Yeah, but that just feels like settling. If I just told myself it was okay to rest, I wouldn't be able to push myself and be successful in school."

"That could happen. I don't know—we haven't tried it. But I also wonder what would happen if you set more realistic expectations for yourself. Maybe it would be easier to regulate your emotions, connect with your classmates, and enjoy the things you do."

"It just scares me. Literally never in my life have I just let myself be."

Now we're getting somewhere as I realize Andrea is thinking about this for the first time. "I'm not saying you can't have goals. You are in med school, Andrea; you do have a lot of responsibilities. But I think the irony is that you are resting anyway. You set these super-high standards for yourself and then can't fulfill them all and then drink to numb the pain of that. It's like when you don't give yourself what you need up front, you will find a way to get your needs met, even if this occurs by drinking so much that you are hungover and sleep all day."

I can tell what I'm saying is resonating with her, but the look on her face appears as though she still hasn't fully understood what I'm saying.

"As much as you want to believe, Andrea, that you are a brain controlling your body and that you can *will* yourself to do anything you want, your body and brain work together. Your body isn't a machine, and you have basic needs that you cannot neglect forever. If you don't give your body rest, your body will demand it. Kind of like your ankle." Andrea shared earlier in the session today that she sprained her ankle as she was training for her most recent marathon. She tried to keep running on it, until she had to go to the ER, where doctors told her she was at risk for causing a fracture if she didn't rest.

"Okay fine, I get it."

"It's impossible to be perfect, Andrea. Rather than continuing to fight with that fact, what if you accepted it and we worked on creating a routine that was actually sustainable? You're going to have to rest anyway, so what if you could enjoy it . . . or at the very least not hate yourself for it?"

"I'm just afraid. I care about being successful," she admits.

"You can take care of yourself and be successful. Responding to your needs and giving yourself breaks doesn't mean you're giving up. The goal is to find a balance in the middle. And have a self-care routine that changes depending on what's going on in your life and how you are feeling. So, during finals, for example, your self-care is going to look different than on break. Your routine will change when you are in the classroom less and with patients more."

"Right. . . . Okay."

"This may be hard for you to do at first because you've used perfectionism and being mean to yourself as a way to motivate yourself."

"Yeah, and my parents did too."

"So, it's kind of like you have been motivating yourself by whipping a donkey. It works fast and it's effective, but over time, your relationship with the donkey erodes and you need to keep whipping harder and harder to get the same result. Just like your relationship with yourself erodes over time. Or we can break this pattern and start using carrots to lure the donkey. We can be kind to the donkey and build trust. It may take longer; the donkey may never be perfect, but over time building a positive relationship with the donkey (and yourself) is more sustainable and leads to better outcomes."

Andrea nods. "Ready to put down your whip?" I ask.

Andrea smirks. "Yes."

What Is Real Self-Care?

So often when I talk to people about self-care, the first thing they think of is bath bombs. I don't totally know how companies like Lush and Bath & Body Works got so lucky, but without fail if you google "self-care," the first thing you see are lists of products to buy. Hopefully, this chapter will change your perception on that.

The truth is a lot of real self-care is *really boring*. It looks like going to the dentist when you don't feel like going, saying no to a trip you cannot afford, turning off your phone, or drinking a glass of water. It's not glamorous. It's not about "treating yourself," and most self-care is not something you can buy. It's not selfish, and contrary to popular belief, you do not have to *earn* your right to practice self-care, just as you don't have to *earn* your right to go to the bathroom or go to sleep each night. Rest and self-care are necessary, and it is impossible to be mentally well without resting. It is important to acknowledge, however, that privilege does impact many individuals' ability to engage in self-care.

A lot of the most important self-care, and the kind that makes the biggest difference in your mental health, is self-care that involves meeting your basic needs. This is because, as we discussed in the previous chapter, your emotional health is completely intertwined with your physical health. Think of Maslow's Hierarchy of Needs. It is really difficult to focus on creating satisfaction and fulfillment in your life if you are struggling to keep a roof over your head and food on the table. And if you do not have access to adequate food, clean drinking water, health care, or safe housing or if you are unable to take a day off from work because you are barely able to keep a roof over your head, it is going to be extremely difficult to meet your basic needs and engage in self-care. This is why when we talk about wellness, mental health, and addiction, it is so important to acknowledge how the role of all types of privilege, not just socioeconomic privilege but also skin tone (white or white passing privilege), gender, cisgender, sexuality, ability, body type, etc., prevents people without such privilege from being able to meet their needs. See the resources listed at the back of the book for more in-depth info by sociologists and people with lived experience about how privilege impacts them and the world.

In recent years, with the internet and social media sharing Maslow's pyramid, his work has been distorted. He never represented his theory as a pyramid; this was actually created post–World War II by a management consultant.[1] Scott Barry Kaufman, psychologist and scholar of Maslow's work states, "Maslow's theory of needs is often presented as a lockstep progression, as though once we satisfy one set of needs, we're done forever with concerning ourselves with the satisfaction of that need. As if life were a video game."[2] People have rightly critiqued this misinterpreted model as lacking cultural competency. The pyramid overly prioritizes individualism, does not account for individual differences, and suggests that psychological needs are less important than physical needs.

It is a sharp contrast to other models of needs, such as the Blackfoot Hierarchy of Needs, known as the Breath of Life Theory, which displays the pyramid in reverse order, with self-actualization at the bottom of the pyramid. The truth is Maslow's own theory was actually very much informed by the Blackfoot culture. He spent several weeks with them on their reservation in Canada and appropriated their understanding of self-actualization for his own model.[3] Kaufman created a more nuanced and updated model of Maslow's work, which is a diagram of a sailboat. In this model, Kaufman is clear that the three needs of the bottom part of the boat are not a hierarchy but work together and are equally important to stabilize the boat. Our basic or security needs include: safety, connection, and self-esteem. These three are important for the boat to be stable and secure. He stresses the importance of security before we can feel comfortable growing, in the same way that a sailboat must have a firm and secure hull before it can open its sail, move, and start exploring. Kaufman writes,

> You don't "climb" a sailboat like you'd climb a mountain or a pyramid. Instead, you open your sail, just like you'd drop your defenses once you felt secure enough. This is an ongoing dynamic: you can be open and spontaneous one minute but can feel threatened enough to prepare for the storm by closing yourself to the world the next minute. The more you continually open yourself to the world, however, the further your boat will go and the more you can benefit from the people and opportunities around you.[4]

The metaphor also works well as it reminds us that we can always pause our growth when we need to slow down, integrate, and get back in touch with more basic needs. Unlike traditional ways of interpreting Maslow's hierarchy, Kaufman argues that all three of these are crucial for security. Therefore, feeling connected to others and feeling a sense of belonging is not just something that is a nice thing to have, it is a basic need. If you have ever heard of Harlow's monkey experiment, you know what I am talking about. In his classic study, psychologist Harry Harlow demonstrated that monkeys preferred a terrycloth "mother" over a wire one, even when the latter provided food. His study demonstrated the importance of affection, touch, and attachment on human development.[5]

Security Needs

Safety Needs (Physiological and Psychological): air, water, food, shelter, sleep, clothing, physical and familial safety, and security

Connection Needs: the need to belong, be liked, and accepted

Self-Esteem Needs: self-esteem, respect of others and self, feeling of accomplishment

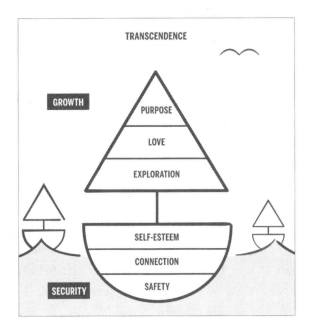

Meeting our needs is never done; it is a process of expanding and contracting depending on what is going on in our life, our mental and physical health, and relationships. The "sail" part of the boat is made up of exploration, love, and purpose, which together provide us with the opportunity of growth and potentially transcendence. Exploration is a very important human need. Our brains are quite literally wired for it; we get a dopamine rush when we engage in new activities and experiences. This was how natural selection shaped us (especially compared to other animals) to become highly adaptable. As Kaufman states, "Engaging in exploration allows us to integrate novel or unexpected events with existing knowledge and experiences, a process necessary for growth."[6] However, if we are not physically or psychologically safe and secure, exploration is not going to be as important to us or enticing. Survival always comes first. We grow from new situations and find joy from exploration when we experience some stress, some uncertainty, some struggle, but not so much that it prevents us from meeting our basic needs. As we discussed in Chapter 3, some stress is healthy for us, but too much stress or chronic stress negatively impacts us. As I lay out the eight different types of self-care, most will include ways to meet our basic, stabilization needs, but I will also include ideas for growth and exploration. Depending on what is going on in your life and how you are feeling, you will determine which part of your sailboat needs your attention.

Types of Self-Care

There are eight types of self-care: emotional, mental, physical, spiritual, social, professional, financial, and environmental. Some of these overlap with one another, but I find it helpful to break it down into these eight categories to give people an understanding and an idea of how expansive, and beyond bath products, real self-care can be. This doesn't mean that you necessarily *need* to engage in self-care of all eight types, however, most of us will see importance and value in doing at least one or two of each category. Many of these suggestions also overlap, so don't get caught up in making sure you hit one from each category. Instead, focus on which ones will support you best depending on what you need. Some of you also may realize through this list that you are doing things that you didn't realize were self-care, in which case, yay! Keep it up.

Emotional

Emotional self-care involves taking action that will take care of your emotional health. As with all these categories, self-care will look different depending on the person. Taking care of your emotional health can positively impact your ability to meet all the needs listed above, since our emotional health is intertwined with almost everything we do. Most of the examples below are ideas that we explored in the last chapter. Flip back for a refresher. We will also cover boundary setting in detail in the next chapter and how to practice self-compassion in Chapter 14.

Examples:

- Noticing how emotions feel in your body (refer back to page 106)
- Sitting with and processing uncomfortable feelings (refer back to page 108)
- Practicing identifying the name of the emotion you are feeling (refer back to page 111)
- Saying "no" + setting boundaries (refer to next chapter)
- Practicing self-compassion (refer to page 220)

Mental

Mental self-care looks like taking action that will support your mental health and state of mind. This is also where learning new skills or challenging yourself in some capacity can support you in meeting your self-esteem needs, as well as those of exploration, love, and purpose.

Examples:

- Read a self-exploration book
- Journal
- Go on a mindful walk
- Learn a new skill
- Host a craft night
- Discover things that you like to do
- Rest or have quiet time
- Do a puzzle
- Paint, draw, sculpt, engage in art in some capacity
- Go to the library
- Travel
- Explore a museum, new restaurant, or area where you live

Physical

Physical self-care involves taking care of yourself physically. It looks like paying attention to what your body needs and what feels good. If you are eating, hydrating, engaging in movement, and sleeping, for example, you'll fulfill safety needs. Dancing, cooking, or getting your hair done will help you fill self-esteem needs or potentially even exploration (if you are trying out a new hair style!).

Examples:

- Dancing
- Eating a fulfilling meal
- Cooking or baking

- Drinking water throughout the day
- Walking outside
- Getting enough sleep
- Stretching
- Taking a shower or bath
- Going to the doctor or dentist
- Getting your nails or hair done or doing a face mask

Spiritual

Spiritual self-care looks like taking action that will support your spirituality. For some this may be religion; for others this may be their individual spiritual beliefs. However even if you are not religious or spiritual, all human beings have a need for meaning and understanding beyond themselves. For some, spiritual self-care may help them meet safety needs if their beliefs give them a sense of safety and security. For others, spiritual self-care may support them in meeting their need for purpose.

Examples:

- Attend a religious gathering
- Join a community group
- Read spiritual texts or share your ideas with others
- Meditate
- Take a nature walk
- Volunteer
- Practice tarot

Social

Social self-care is one of the most important types of self-care we can engage in because connection to others is a crucial need we all have.

It can look different for different people depending on how much connection we have built into our lives (if you live alone or with people or work from home versus going to an office) and our levels of extraversion. With the rise of social media, we have the capacity to be connected to more people than ever, but as a result, we are developing fewer deep connections with friends. Seeing people in person can often fulfill us on a deeper level, even if we do not know people very well. Engaging in social care allows us to meet our need for connection, self-esteem, exploration (as we meet new friends), and love.

Examples:

- Schedule a phone call with a long-distance friend
- Spend time with family or friends
- Go on a double date
- Go for a walk with a friend
- Get to know your neighbors
- Join a book club or any group that interests you
- Go to a dog park or take your kids to play on a playground
- Join an online group that caters to your particular interests
- Unfollow people on social media who lead you to feel lonely or bad about yourself

Professional

Professional self-care involves taking action to support your career, vocation, or professional life. It is important in meeting your safety and self-esteem needs but also may support you in meeting your need for connection as well as purpose. Furthermore, engaging in professional self-care supports you in being able to take care of your mental health by ensuring you do not burn out at work and are able to continue to feel fulfilled by your job.

Examples:

- Schedule stretching breaks
- Set boundaries with coworkers
- Eat a nourishing lunch away from your desk or workspace
- Attend professional development trainings
- Be punctual
- Ask for help or clarification
- Share your ideas with your team

Financial

Financial self-care looks like taking action that will support you in meeting your financial goals and protecting your resources. This type of self-care allows us to meet our safety needs and increase our self-esteem.

Examples:

- Pay your bills on time
- Create (and stick to!) a budget
- Eat meals at home
- Cancel automatic subscriptions
- Use public transit
- Unsubscribe from emails that promote shopping and entice with coupons
- Spend money on things that bring you joy or fill a need
- Meet with a financial planner

Environmental

Environmental self-care looks like taking action that takes care of the environment or space that you reside in. For most of us, the space we spend time in can have an impact on how we feel. Having physical reminders of things that we are avoiding, such as putting away laundry or dishes, can make us feel overwhelmed.

Examples:

- Keep common spaces clutter free
- Tidy up regularly
- Create a weekly cleaning schedule
- Decorate your space in a way that feels nourishing
- Create a routine around chores
- Change your sheets
- Decorate your desk at work

As you can see, true self-care does not always look like doing things that are necessarily fun. Things like going to the doctor or dentist are not fun but are some of the best things you can do to engage in physical self-care. The difficult part about self-care is that it looks different for everyone and changes depending on the situation and your stage of life. What looks like self-care for a young adult is very different than for someone who has children. It is going to look different if you didn't sleep last night because you were up with a crying baby versus if you just moved to a new city. In the former case, sleep will likely be a priority versus, in the latter, self-care may be engaging in social activities and making new friends. Give up the idea that your self-care routine will always look the same. As you grow, change, and enter new stages of life, so will your self-care routine.

If you are struggling to identify if something is self-care for you, I recommend asking yourself "how will I feel after I do this?" Not during—because for some of us, we may not like cleaning or going to the dentist—but after you complete the task. If you push yourself to exercise when you are drained and tired, you will feel worse a few hours later. If you push yourself to go out and see friends when you need to catch up on work, you will not feel better. However, if you are feeling anxious about going on a first date but are committed to finding a relationship, you will likely feel *better* and proud of yourself for going (even if the date doesn't work out). Self-care is about taking care of your future self. But this does not necessarily mean that your future self always needs you to do more. Many times, taking a nap, skipping a workout, or setting a boundary are something your future self will thank you for. You can see this example clearly with Andrea and her ankle.

Only you can know for sure. If you are someone who leans toward overfunctioning, your self-care will probably look a lot like slowing down, resting, and asking for help. If you are someone who gets overwhelmed and underfunctions during times of stress, your work will be to commit to taking small action, following through, and keeping small promises to yourself *even when you really don't feel like doing it.* You may over- or underfunction in different areas of your life. I encourage you to experiment, to try different things, and to notice what truly nourishes you. Expect yourself to mess up and treat yourself with kindness and self-compassion when you do. This isn't a race and there is no perfect self-care routine. Remember that self-care is a tool of reparenting, so treating yourself like a loving parent is a helpful guidepost in discovering what actions are true self-care for you.

Questions to Help You Discover If Something Is Self-Care

- Do I have enough energy to do this right now?
- How do I feel?
- How will I feel after I finish?
- Will I have more or less energy after I finish?
- Is it worth the energy expenditure?

- Is it worth the financial cost?
- What happens if I don't do it?
- Is there a smaller step I can take in this process?
- Is there something I can do first to give me more energy?
- Are my primary needs taken care of?
- Am I taking this action out of choice or as a reaction to something?
- If I delay and wait twenty minutes, will my choice be different?
- Does this action feel compulsive?

Chapter 10

Boundaries

**When you say yes to others, make sure you
aren't saying no to yourself.**

—Paulo Coelho

"Okay, I think you are right. I need boundaries," Brianna tells me at the beginning of her session.

"Oh yeah?" I say and I am genuinely surprised. Not that she needs boundaries, of course, as I don't think I have encountered a mother who doesn't need boundaries. But I am surprised that she changed her mind about this so quickly. In the past, when I have brought this up, she has brushed it off. "What happened?" I ask.

"Well, I noticed my daughter Mia has been acting differently lately. She used to be so bubbly and lately she's been quieter. She has become like my shadow. Following me around the house. I thought maybe it was just because she was adjusting to her new school. I asked her if she wanted to have a playdate with some of her new friends and she said no. She was following me around so much yesterday, I snapped. I couldn't take it. I just needed a second alone. I yelled at her and she started hysterically crying and wouldn't talk to me. I don't want that to happen again."

"That's so hard, Brianna," I say gently. "Being a parent is really difficult."

"Yeah. I just feel like this is a wake-up call. I think you're right. I really can't do everything I'm doing. I cannot work from home and have two kids hanging on me 24/7. I already have my youngest who isn't in school yet. I was hoping for some relief when Mia started kindergarten. I know I need boundaries, but I feel terrible about it. I keep thinking, why do I need boundaries from my little girl?"

"Brianna, you are a mother, yes, but you are also a human. Needing some time alone or space from your kids does not mean you don't love them."

"Yeah, I guess. I just have always prided myself on 'doing it all' and not needing any outside help. I feel like even if I am dying inside it's better for my kids to have a clean house and have me around even if I wasn't all there emotionally."

"You aren't superwoman, Brianna. It is going to be literally impossible to not have moments when you get upset and overwhelmed and take it out on your kids. The point of motherhood is not to be perfect. You do the best you can and apologize when you mess up and try to do better. But boundaries can make it a lot easier to be emotionally present with your kids. And boundaries will definitely make it easier for you to stop drinking."

"I know you're right. I just feel like as a mother this is what I'm supposed to do. I should be able to sacrifice everything for my kids. I shouldn't need time alone."

"When you think about Mia, and her life when she grows up, what do you want for her?"

"I want her to find someone she loves and who takes care of her. I want her to have a job she finds fulfilling. But mostly I want her to be happy."

"Are you happy?"

"I love my kids, but I feel like I'm dying inside." Brianna slumps forward.

"I have a hard question for you," I say. Brianna looks up. "Would you want this life for Mia?"

Tears start to roll down Brianna's face. She shakes her head.

"This is really important," I say. "So many parents don't realize this until their children are adults, or until their kids start modeling their parents' lack of boundaries or self-care or people-pleasing tendencies. And our society really overestimates how parenting looks on the outside and underestimates how parenting feels for parents and kids. There is this idea that being a good mother looks like sacrificing yourself for your kids and being a martyr. But the truth is, children learn more from modeling than from anything else. And if we want our children to grow up to be authentic and honest and not tolerate being treated poorly, we have to be authentic and treat ourselves well too. It's healthy for children to see parents setting boundaries and taking care of themselves. It teaches children how to do this."

"Yeah," Brianna says. "I just don't know how I am going to do this. I feel guilty even thinking about the *idea* of setting boundaries."

"Well, what is a boundary that you would like to set?" I ask.

"I would love to hire a nanny to watch the kids after school for a few hours a few times a week. I feel weird hiring someone when my in-laws have offered, but they are not great at keeping the kids' routine. And I just really need reliable support."

"I think that sounds like a really good idea. Motherhood is hard enough as it is. It is impossible to do without help, especially when you and your husband work full-time."

"I work from home."

"You work full-time, Brianna. Don't discount how difficult it is to work full-time and take care of the kids when they come home from school. You also have a four-year-old who doesn't go to school yet."

Brianna lets out a sigh. "Okay, you're right. I just feel so guilty."

"Here's the thing, though. You already feel guilty for thinking about this. You are going to feel guilt for wanting to do this. So, if you are going to feel guilty either way, let's start by setting this boundary and taking care of you. Boundaries are a skill. So we practice them and feel less guilty through taking action. As we implement them, we feel less guilty over time as we see how they positively impact us and those around us."

"Okay, where do we begin?"

What Style of Boundaries Do You Have?

First, let's define what a boundary is. A boundary is an internally created guideline or limit that a person creates in order to identify what are appropriate or safe ways for others to act around you. This may include what topics of conversation you will discuss, whether you lend money to others, or what kind of physical touch is acceptable. Boundaries are also distinct from demands because they are created based on what works for you rather than with the intention of trying to force someone else to do something or behave in a specific way. Healthy boundaries can also be molded, changed, and negotiated depending on how important a boundary is for us or how close we are with a person. For example, we may have to negotiate some of our boundaries

Demands	Boundaries	Requests
• Based on trying to control or limit another	• Guideline or limit that a person creates to identify what are reasonable, safe, and acceptable ways for others to behave around themselves	• Asserting a want or need respectfully
• A forceful statement that something must be done and there is no negotiation	• Outside your hard boundaries; you may be able to tolerate negotiation on what those specific boundaries look like or how they are carried out	• Able to tolerate the denial or request and negotiate if needed
• Denial is not acceptable	• Created by you; not needing anyone's involvement	• The act of asking for something

with a partner or spouse in order to compromise and have both individuals' needs met.

In order to help us figure out how and where to set boundaries in our lives, it's important to understand that there are a few styles of boundaries that we may have. The three styles are **rigid**, **healthy**, and **porous**. Think of it as a spectrum, with rigid boundaries being the firmest and strongest, and porous boundaries being the loosest, most open, or ineffectively expressed. Porous boundaries often cause us to say yes when we want to say no, leading us to feel resentful toward others. Then we end up exploding or acting in a passive-aggressive manner later. The goal is to have healthy boundaries as much as possible. Healthy boundaries allow us to have authentic and intimate connections with other people, where we understand what one another's needs, limits, and values are, and we respect them. We may not know this up front, but we learn along the way, and this allows us to build trust.

Boundaries are not selfish. They teach people how to treat us and show people what our needs, wants, and limitations are. As Brené Brown says, "Clear is kind. Unclear is unkind."[1] The truth is, if we avoid conflict or being honest with others about our thoughts or expectations, we are setting people up to fail. People are unable to read our minds. Expecting people to be able to know what we want or need breeds resentment, gossip, dishonesty, and blame, all of which create even larger conflicts down the road. Contrary to popular belief, boundaries actually enhance our relationships with other people. Most people who set boundaries with us are doing it because they actually value and want a relationship with us. Keep this in mind throughout this chapter and as you start to set boundaries. When someone sets a boundary with you, it is actually a compliment, and setting a boundary shows how important that person is to you. However, I do want to note that we cannot set healthy boundaries with people who do not respect them. Therefore, depending on which people and areas of your life you are focusing on, if someone will not respect your boundaries repeatedly, it may actually be healthier to have a rigid boundary in order to keep yourself safe.

Think of boundaries as doors. As relationship coach Mark Groves says, "Walls keep everyone out. Boundaries teach people where the door is."[2] To continue with the door metaphor, I like to say that rigid boundaries are like a thick wooden door. Things cannot get in or out of it, but unlike a wall, you can choose to open the door and let someone in. Porous boundaries are the equivalent of a door with large holes in it. Things can come in and out but only in certain spots and often we don't have control over how quickly or how much comes out. Finally, healthy boundaries are like a screen door.

You can filter what comes in and out while also being flexible (since the screen has some give to it) as needed. The screen, like healthy boundaries, allows you to be discerning of who can come in and out of your life and what you tolerate or not, depending on your past experiences, needs, and values.

It is also important to understand that you can have different styles of boundaries depending on different areas of your life. For example, when it comes to Brianna's children, she has porous boundaries. She doesn't often make time for herself and struggles to say no to doing things for them. This leads her to feel frustrated, burned out, and resentful because she has such high expectations for herself that when she inevitably cannot meet them, she yells at her kids. Her door has holes in it, and this leads to her leaking her frustration all over her children. If she starts setting more healthy boundaries with her kids and hires a sitter, she will be able to be more emotionally present with her kids and less likely to snap at them. However, when it comes to Brianna's extended family, she has feelings of abandonment from when her father died and struggles with trusting they will be there for her. Thus, she tends to have rigid boundaries with her extended family and keeps them at a distance. Brianna has healthy boundaries with her husband. They have excellent communication and are able to work through disagreements, compromise, and say no to each other.

Let's dive deeper into some common ways that these three different boundary styles manifest. As you read through these, remember that you can also have different boundaries with different people in your life. Most people have a mix of rigid, porous, and healthy boundaries depending on the person and situation. The goal is to help you identify where you have these different types of boundaries and how it impacts you so that you can take action to create as many healthy boundaries as possible.

Some Signs You May Have Rigid Boundaries

- You become aggressive or give people the silent treatment when frustrated with them
- You are extremely independent
- You were raised in a family where keeping things "in the family" was highly important
- Some may describe you as detached, protective, mysterious, or closed-off
- You never witnessed your parents or caregivers engage in healthy conflict as a child. Everything happened behind closed doors
- Your caregivers often gave the reason of "because I said so" when they set a boundary or limit with you
- You have a history of cutting people off if someone does something that upsets you

Rigid Boundaries Look Like . . .

- Avoiding close relationships
- Avoiding vulnerability
- Cutting people off or ghosting people at the first sign of conflict
- Being unable to ask for help
- Having extremely high expectations of others
- Struggling to trust people
- Keeping others at a distance to avoid the possibility of rejection

Some Signs You May Have Porous Boundaries

- You often feel guilty and responsible for how others feel
- You feel resentful of others, especially when they ask for what they need

- You sometimes expect people to read your mind or know what you want
- You struggle to voice your opinion
- You feel like people continuously break their word with you
- You become passive-aggressive when frustrated
- You feel overwhelmed with all your responsibilities
- You feel resentful when you see people ask for what they need
- You avoid people if you suspect they are going to ask you to do something because you fear you won't be able to say no
- You often feel like you give people too many chances

Porous Boundaries Look Like . . .

- Struggling to say no or people pleasing
- Oversharing
- Often needing to explain or justify your decision when you say no
- Being overly involved in other's issues
- Not being able to keep secrets or keep things private
- Accepting mistreatment or abuse
- Feeling dependent on another person's approval or acceptance
- Struggling to make decisions without consulting others
- Your parents or caregivers struggled to say no to you or your siblings and set limits

Some Signs You Have Healthy Boundaries

- You may not like saying no to people, but you understand that it's important so that you can take care of yourself
- If someone pushes back when you say no, you understand this doesn't mean you should have said yes

- If someone negatively responds to something you said, you don't automatically assume that you did something wrong
- When someone shares something with you, you do not automatically reciprocate
- You feel comfortable standing up for yourself when needed

Healthy Boundaries Look Like . . .

- Being able to say no
- Respecting others when they say no
- Being able to maintain your own sense of self while listening to other people's perspectives
- Honestly and clearly communicating with others (especially in regard to your expectations of them and your own limits)
- Not compromising on your own values for others
- Being able to shift your boundaries and compromise depending on the situation and person

The goal of healthy boundaries is to find a middle ground where your boundaries are flexible yet firm and allow you to adapt depending on the situation. You'll want to firm up porous boundaries and relax more rigid ones.

Let's look at how these three styles of boundaries may show up in the same situation so you can see the difference. Since this is a book about your relationship with alcohol, let's take the example that you are on your sober journey and you are offered a drink. If you have porous boundaries in this situation, it will likely be hard for you to say no. You may feel guilty about disappointing this person and you may say yes and think to yourself, *Well, I will just start over again tomorrow, no big deal.* Or you could feel tempted to say yes to this person but then pretend to sip your drink in order to avoid stating your boundaries. On the other hand, having a rigid boundary may sound like making a passive-aggressive or aggressive comment and/or cutting this person out of your life for not remembering you were trying to stop drinking. An example of a healthy boundary in this situation would be telling your friend, "No thank you. I'm actually not drinking right now. I'm not sure when I plan on drinking again, so it would help me if you didn't ask me again."

Types of Boundaries

Now that we have broken down the different styles of boundaries, let's talk about the different types of boundaries. There are six main types of boundaries: **material**, **physical**, **temporal**, **sexual**, **mental**, and **emotional**. In every section, I give examples of common ways our boundaries get violated. If we have a history of having certain boundaries violated, or a history of trauma, we may be more sensitive to boundary violations or need firmer boundaries in order to take care of ourselves in the future. It's common for boundary violations to have happened when we were children as well, which means it will be even more important for us to take care of ourselves now that we are adults. This is why boundaries are such an important component of reparenting.

As you read through these examples, it is likely you will relate to many in different categories. This does not necessarily mean that something is wrong with how you were raised. Most of our caregivers were not raised with boundaries. Our society and culture do not prioritize and respect people's boundaries. We live in a culture where gaslighting,* catcalling, forcing children to hug adults, microaggressions, and pretending

---

* Gaslighting is when someone attempts to manipulate you by telling you that your perception or ideas of something is not true. It derives from the 1944 movie *Gaslight*, in which a man makes his wife doubt her sanity by lying to her when she raises concerns that there is something wrong with their house. He calls her forgetful and makes her question her own sanity.

everything is okay are often the norm. It's rare to encounter families, systems, and organizations where meetings start and end on time, consent is explicitly discussed, and people take responsibility for mistakes and accept feedback. I believe this is especially important to point out because normal boundary conversations tend to overemphasize the importance of personal responsibility; when in fact, boundaries are difficult for us to implement and follow through with because our culture does not tolerate or respect many types of boundaries. You may also read through this list and notice times where you violated other people's boundaries. That's okay. This is why you are reading this book. Learn from this list, take accountability when you violate someone's boundaries, and do better in the future. It doesn't mean you are a bad person.

Material boundaries are often the easiest to understand. They refer to boundaries around our material possessions. This can be something as small as a water bottle but also includes things like whether you allow people into your home as well. Material boundaries can also refer to boundaries you have with yourself around your technology or other possessions. These can also be helpful with children, as you get to decide, for example, what toys they get to play with at home or how much screen time they are allowed.

Ways Our Material Boundaries Are Violated:

- Someone steals or borrows something from you without your permission
- Someone gives you a gift when you ask them not to
- Someone gives you a bag of donations after you tell them you do not want them
- Someone sends you care packages with food they know you cannot eat
- Someone eats food off your plate without your permission

Examples of Material Boundaries:

- Not lending money
- Not accepting physical gifts
- Not having a TV in your bedroom
- Not sharing clothing
- Not letting someone else drive your car
- Only letting close friends stay in your home
- Not letting someone sleep in your bed
- Not sharing food
- Not letting your partner go through your phone without your permission

Physical boundaries refer to limits around physical touch and your space. It can also involve who you spend time with and feel safe around in addition to what places and areas you physically go. It is healthy and normal to have different boundaries with different people in your life depending on your closeness and comfort. One of the best things we can teach children is that they have a right to their body and to physical space. Parents and caregivers can do this by allowing their children to choose if they want to hug or give physical affection, and if so, to whom, and knocking when entering their rooms and providing privacy, especially as children get older. If you have a history of trauma, even if it may not feel as though there was a clear "physical boundary violation," you may also find yourself needing more physical space from others or feeling more uncomfortable with physical touch.

Everyone is different and has their own comfort level with touch. If you are someone who lives in a body that is often ignored, discounted, or violated, whether explicitly (by touching you) or implicitly (by not being able to use a bathroom on a plane due to your body size), it is also likely you will need firmer physical boundaries and may be more aware of when they are violated. There is nothing right or wrong about how much touch or closeness you feel comfortable with. Do not allow someone to tell you that you are being "sensitive." You get to choose what works for you based on how systems and the world impact you. If you are in a marginalized group, you may not feel comfortable going certain places if you feel as though you are physically at risk. While this is not fair, and our society needs to do more to protect those with the least power, I want you to know that you have a right to take care of yourself and do what works for you. You are not "overreacting" just because others (especially individuals with more privilege) don't understand your physical boundaries.

Ways Our Physical Boundaries Are Violated:

- Being forced to hug, kiss, or touch family members or other people when we were young
- Being physically abused
- Being deprived of physical touch (especially as a child)
- Being hugged by teachers, mentors, therapists, friends, strangers, etc., without our consent
- Being poked, touched, or tickled after telling someone to stop
- If you are someone with a physical disability, not being able to use a public bathroom, find an elevator, find a ramp, etc.
- If you are someone in a fat* body, not being able to sit in a chair in public, eat at a restaurant, sit on a plane, on a bus, get in an MRI machine, etc., because your body is not accommodated

---

* I use the word "fat" not as an insult but as a neutral descriptor as part of the fat positivity movement and body neutrality movement where fat people reclaim the word "fat" as a neutral descriptor of their body type. For more information, check out the resources I've listed in the back of the book.

- When adults tell children they have to finish their plate, forcing them to eat past fullness or when adults don't allow children to have more food or have snacks when they are hungry
- If a stranger or anybody purposefully touches your body without permission; while being touched by a stranger is a boundary violation for almost any of us, sometimes this can even be a microaggression, for example, when a non-Black person touches the hair of a Black woman

Examples of Physical Boundaries:

- Not shaking hands with strangers
- Only hugging people in your family
- Needing personal space while sitting on the couch with others
- Asking people to knock when your door is closed
- Only sharing a bed with your partner
- Not going to certain restaurants or public places where you are unsure if your body will be treated with respect and dignity
- Skipping an event because you don't feel safe being around someone there
- Not sitting close to someone in a public place if possible, due to the potential of being touched
- Not going to certain places that you feel uncomfortable with

Temporal (time) boundaries have to do with how much time and energy we spend with others and ourselves. Having healthy time boundaries allows us to be able to take care of ourselves and have our time respected by others. It also includes accounting for what drains us or takes a lot of energy and allows us to say no to certain things, so we can say yes to other things that are more important to us.

Ways Our Temporal Boundaries Are Violated:

- People insist we stay longer at a meeting, event, gathering, etc.
- People give you a hard time and try to guilt you into staying longer than you said you could
- Scheduled events, appointments, or classes do not start or end on time
- People ask for support from you but do not return the favor; they do not inquire about your life or support you in the same way
- People do not accept when you say you do not have the time or energy to do something
- Your job often forces you to work late or work longer hours than agreed upon without compensation or consent

Examples of Temporal Boundaries:

- Not staying late after work
- Setting limits on time you spend with people who are chronically late or cancel often
- Scheduling time to be alone versus time to spend with others
- Not participating in one-sided relationships
- Scheduling time to recover after doing things that are draining
- Saying no when you don't have the time or energy to do something

Sexual boundaries include what you are willing to do sexually. This not only includes what sexual acts and types of sexual touch you will engage in and with whom but also conversations around sexuality. Consent and contraception are really important sexual boundaries, and also boundaries around what is considered cheating with a partner.

Ways Our Sexual Boundaries Are Violated:

- If you were sexually abused, raped, molested, or sexually harassed
- Catcalled or told to "smile" by a stranger (especially a man saying this to a woman)
- Someone makes an inappropriate sexual remark to you
- Someone sends you a picture of their genitals or a naked picture of themselves or someone else without your consent
- Someone pressures, bullies, or tries to cajole you into doing certain sexual acts whether this is explicitly said or implied
- Someone does not ask for consent to do something sexually to you
- Someone does not use protection when having sex

Examples of Sexual Boundaries:

- Asking for consent
- Discussing contraception
- Not feeling comfortable with PDA
- Saying no to sexual acts that you are not comfortable with
- Not allowing people to call you certain sexual names
- Having a safe word
- Discussing what you consider is cheating

Mental boundaries primarily refer to what topics of conversation you are willing to engage in and with whom. They also involve what thoughts and ideas you are willing to talk about. This can also extend to who you engage with online or what types of accounts or topics you follow. Having someone attempt to gaslight us is often a common way our mental boundary gets violated. If you are a person with a marginalized identity, you have a right to not engage with certain people who do not respect your mental boundaries or make you feel crazy for asking people to stop saying comments that are microaggressions.* This is a change that needs to happen from a societal perspective. Until that happens, you have a right to protect yourself as needed.

Ways Our Mental Boundaries Are Violated:

- Gaslighting
- If you grew up in a household where adults did not acknowledge when something was going on. For example, if someone was often drunk or a caregiver left the household, and it was not discussed or acknowledged.
- Your parents or caregivers had rules around what was allowed to be talked about, e.g., "What happens in the home stays in the home"
- Your experience, opinions, ideas, or thoughts were continuously invalidated, leading you to question yourself
- Being told you are "crazy" or "don't know what you're talking about"
- Multiple perspectives or ideas were not tolerated in your household growing up
- Microaggressions

Examples of Mental Boundaries:

- Not engaging in certain topics of conversation around certain people
- Not engaging in a serious discussion in a crowded bar, where you can't hear the person

---

* A microaggression is a statement, action, or incident regarded as an instance of indirect, subtle, or unintentional discrimination against members of a marginalized group, such as a racial or ethnic minority.

- Not talking about certain topics at work
- Not debating strangers on social media
- Not following certain people or engaging with them on social media
- Staying true to your own values and beliefs even around others who disagree
- Not engaging with people who gaslight you

Emotional boundaries entail whether we share certain personal information with others or how quickly we open up. They also look like being mindful of your emotions and asking for a break during a heated argument or not having certain conversations in public for privacy. Emotional boundaries also involve our ability to not take on other people's emotions as our own. If your family or caregivers often did not acknowledge their own emotions or yours, these may be more difficult for you. If you are in a marginalized group, it also (unfortunately) may look like you choosing to not go to certain places in order to ensure you won't be bullied, harassed, or teased. This is not fair, and our systems need to change so that the burden of protecting oneself is not always on those with the least power.

Ways Our Emotional Boundaries Are Violated:

- Parents or caregivers treated you like their therapist or friend while you were growing up
- Parents or caregivers triangulate you and put you in the middle of their relationship
- People vent or unload their struggles on you without asking if you have the capacity to listen and be present with them
- People gossip or talk about other people you are close with, putting you in the middle

- People are not emotionally present or validating when you share something deeply emotional or sensitive
- People are not acknowledging their or your emotions. Especially in a family, the mantra may be to not talk about feelings
- Being neglected emotionally by your parents or caregivers
- Being shamed or bullied for any reason, especially for your weight, gender, sexual orientation, race, ability, clothes, religion, etc.
- Emotional manipulation
- People using God, religion, or spirituality as a way to control you or get you to do what they want

Examples of Emotional Boundaries:

- Needing time to cool off after an argument
- Not allowing people to shame or belittle you
- Not trying to fix your parents' relationship
- Not answering personal questions if you don't know someone very well
- Not taking on other people's emotions as your responsibility if they react negatively to you setting a boundary
- Asking someone if you can revisit the conversation when you are in a better mood
- Not going to certain local venues or areas of the country or world where you are unsure if you will be bullied, harassed, or made fun of due to your race, gender, sexual orientation, class, religion, ability, weight, etc. This would be a boundary with yourself.
- Not talking about religion with certain people

How to Communicate Your Boundaries

Hopefully by now you are getting a sense of what boundaries you may want and need. Remember: boundaries, especially healthy ones, can be changed and modified as needed. Try not to put pressure on yourself to set the perfect boundary or to know exactly what you want. As we get into this section, also remember that if you don't fully communicate your boundary in one conversation, that is okay too. Sometimes it takes a few conversations to get your point across. Boundaries need to be maintained over time. Just like you may need to clean or repaint your door, you will need to put work in to make sure your boundaries with others stay healthy and true to what you need depending on what is going on in your life.

Some of the boundaries I outlined above are boundaries that you will create with yourself. Therefore, it will not involve talking to another person about your boundary. You practice setting boundaries with yourself by brainstorming from the list above and taking action. Then, you modify or change your boundary as needed. Self-boundaries are very similar to self-care. They include doing things like not keeping a TV in your bedroom, having a bedtime, sticking to a budget, or unfollowing people on social media who negatively impact your mood.

Boundaries are often divided into two parts: setting a limit and stating a consequence. While I understand the logic of saying that, I also want to let you know that you have a right to choose how you set boundaries. We may have stricter boundaries with stricter consequences depending on how many times we have set a boundary and how close we are to the person. If this is your first time sharing with someone that you don't want them to talk about X, it may not be helpful to immediately state a consequence if they break your boundary. However, if it is a situation that keeps arising, it is important to set a consequence, so that people can make an informed choice about the impact their actions will have on you. Let's look at some common examples to set boundaries for people you do not know well or those who you want to set very strict boundaries with.

Examples:

- **Material:** "Please do not take my pen without asking. If you do this again, I am not going to be able to study with you."
- **Physical:** "I am not comfortable with you touching my hair. I am not going to be able to spend time with you if you cannot respect this boundary."
- **Temporal:** "I only have twenty minutes to talk on the phone. After that, I need to go spend time with my family."
- **Sexual:** "I do not have sex without using protection. If you continue to ask me to do this, we are not going to be able to spend time together anymore."
- **Mental:** "Please do not talk about my weight. If you continue to make comments like this, I will not be able to spend time with you."
- **Emotional:** "I do not feel comfortable answering that question. Please do not ask me again. If you continue to ask me this, I won't be able to share intimate details of my life with you."

If you are setting a boundary with someone you have a relationship with—whether that is a friend, partner, family member, colleague, or parent—you may get pushback if you simply state the boundary as outlined above. People may want to defend themselves and share how their intentions were good. People may be offended or not understand where this boundary is "coming from." They may say that they feel you are being mean or rude. People in general tend to resist change and like to keep the status quo. This doesn't mean that there is anything wrong with your boundaries. However, I find there are some simple ways to make people more receptive and understanding of your boundaries by changing some phrasing and providing context. This can be accomplished through either acknowledging that the boundary is new and/or a change from the status quo of the relationship or stating that you understand that they have good intentions. If it is also your first time setting a boundary with someone, you have the option to *not* set a consequence and instead see if they respect your boundary first. This will also depend on how important this boundary is to you. As you identify the different types of boundaries you want and need, I also recommend deciding what is your nonnegotiable bottom line, and where you can compromise. If you can compromise in a boundary, you have the option to provide an alternative to someone rather than simply stating what they cannot do.

Acknowledge: "I know in the past I have not said anything about X. However, I am realizing I am actually uncomfortable with it."

Understand: "I know you love me/care about me/have good intentions when you say or do X. At the same time, it does not work for me when you say or do X."

State the Boundary: "Please do not do or say X."

Set the Limit or Offer an Alternative: "If you do X again, I will do Y." Or "Could we do Y instead?"

Examples:

- **Material:** "I know in the past I have been fine with sharing clothes. However, I'm working on boundaries and realizing that I am actually uncomfortable with it. Please do not ask if you can borrow my clothes in the future."

- **Physical:** "I know you love me and care about me, which is why you want to be close to me. However, I need some physical space right now from sitting so close to you on the couch."
- **Temporal:** "I love how close we are. At the same time, I get overwhelmed when you call me a few times in a row. I unfortunately do not have time to talk on the phone every day. How about we set up a recurring time to chat once a week?"
- **Sexual:** "I know you want to hold my hand in public because you care about me and are proud to be with me. At the same time, I am really uncomfortable with PDA. I am happy to hold your hand at home or in private."
- **Mental:** "I know you love me, but at the same time, I have different political beliefs than you. I am not comfortable talking about politics and will need to limit the time I spend with you if you continue to talk about them."
- **Emotional:** "Mom and Dad, I know I haven't spoken up in the past, but the truth is I am realizing it is very uncomfortable for me to hear you vent about each other. Please seek outside support. I am happy to talk to you guys about anything else, but I can no longer be in the middle."

Boundaries are a skill, one that most of us unfortunately do not learn about until we are adults. Be patient with yourself on this journey and know that the more you practice it, the easier it will get. Many of us use alcohol as a way to numb the discomfort or pain of having our boundaries continuously crossed. Brianna uses alcohol to cope with the pain of not setting boundaries with her kids.

Boundaries are essential for our mental health. In order to engage in real self-care, honor your emotions, and reparent yourself, you will need to learn how to set boundaries. Therefore, learning how to set

**If you don't drink,
you may need these boundaries...**

- Not keeping alcohol in your home
- Not going to bars or restaurants where you used to get drunk
- Not spending time with "drinking buddies"
- Taking a different route home so that you don't drive past the bar
you used to frequent after work
- Setting a limit with how much time you spend with family members
- Not watching certain TV shows or movies that glorify drinking
- Unfollow drinking friends on social media
- Instructing friends to not invite you to go out drinking with them

boundaries and maintain them is a crucial part of changing your relationship with alcohol. You may also need some specific boundaries with yourself and others that will help make getting sober a bit easier.

Hopefully by this point, you are beginning to see how **mindfulness, emotional regulation, self-care**, and **boundaries** (the four tools of reparenting) are interconnected and reinforce each other. If we are unable to differentiate between ourselves and the voice in our head, we will struggle to identify and process our emotions. If we cannot identify and process our emotions, we will struggle to properly take the action that will lead us to feel better. And finally, if we cannot take care of ourselves effectively, we will struggle to articulate to others how they can and may treat us and enforce consequences if they do not act appropriately. These four tools are important because, if we do not engage in this reparenting work, we will struggle to heal our relationship with alcohol or any other addictive or unhealthy pattern because we are not getting to the root of the issue. (Remember that first outer layer of the iceberg?) If you find yourself still struggling with boundaries, you may need to dig a little deeper into your history and relationship with boundaries. I recommend journaling about some of the questions below. Sometimes understanding *why* you may be struggling with boundaries will lead you to being able to answer *what* boundaries you need, *where* you need them, and *who* you need to set them with.

Exercise: Grab a sheet of paper and a pen and answer the following questions.

1. Where did I first learn about boundaries?
2. Did my caregivers model healthy boundaries for me when I was growing up?
3. Did my caregivers respect my wishes to not spend time with or not be friends with certain kids when I was young?
4. How did they handle it when I said no or stated preferences?
5. Did my teachers or adults model healthy boundaries?
6. How did they react to me saying no or stating preferences?

Part 3

Make It Stick

How to Build a Life You Don't Need to Escape From

Chapter 11

One Thing at a Time

There is only one way to eat an elephant—a bite at a time.

—Desmond Tutu

Brianna sashays into my office with the biggest smile on her face. "Sixty days today!!"

"Ahh, congrats!" I beam. "I'm so glad you feel proud. I know you've struggled with feeling like you deserve to celebrate this."

"I feel like I am hitting my stride. I never thought I would say this, but setting boundaries has really been a game changer for me."

"Good!" I say, "and what self-care have you been able to do since setting boundaries?"

"Well, I've been going to the gym. I hired a personal trainer. She says that if I stick to the workout routine and meal plan she created, she thinks I will be able to get back to my pre-baby weight."

"I'm glad you are feeling good and taking time for yourself. What does the meal plan and workout routine look like?"

As Brianna lays out the elaborate workout schedule and meal plan, filled with supplements and intermittent fasting, a knot forms in my stomach. I see this pattern so often with individuals once they stop drinking. Typically, it goes one of two ways. One—someone feels so good about not drinking they want to start cutting out any habit or pattern they see as unhealthy or negative. While this client's motives are in the right place, this quest often becomes sticky at best, as the goal of perfection is unattainable. At worst, they will end up burned out with another addictive behavior that we will have to work on, such as chronic dieting, excessive exercising, binging, purging, restriction, an obsession with "clean eating" (all the makings of an eating disorder), workaholism, and/or perfectionism. Sometimes individuals even go so far as to become obsessed with tanning, Botox, cosmetic surgery, or procedures in a never-ending desire to look perfect.

The second pattern occurs when a person straight up replaces their drinking with another addictive behavior. This can look like shopping, gambling, compulsive sex or dating, self-harm, or switching to another addictive substance (like drugs). In both cases, the individual does not do the inner work in order to heal the root causes of their drinking. They simply find another habit or substance to fill the hole that sobriety has left. While the individual may temporarily be able to stay sober, eventually most of us go back to our preferred vice, whether that is alcohol or something else.

Think back to the iceberg metaphor. Only 15 percent of an iceberg represents the symptom. The other 85 percent of the iceberg consists of two layers. The outer layer consists of the more easily identified issues that individuals use alcohol to cope with, such as anxiety, depression, low self-esteem, shame, fear, disconnection, cognitive fusion, and helplessness. Under that is the core layer, which directly spawns the outer layer. The core layer is made up of trauma, family history of addiction, biological predisposition (genetics), environmental factors, and structural and systemic inequalities (health care, housing, income, education) as a result of race, gender, ability, religion, sexual orientation, and class. The more boxes you have checked, the more susceptible you are to develop an issue with alcohol or another addictive pattern.

For example, as a Black woman, Brianna is more likely to experience structural inequalities and have less access to good health care,

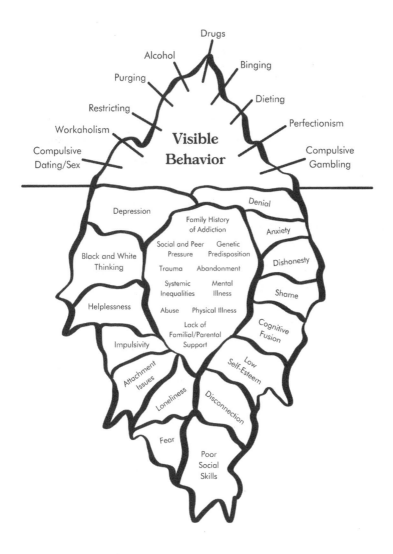

safe housing, economic and job security, and education than a white individual. As a woman, she is likely to make less money than a man doing the same job as her, and as a mother, she is more likely to take on a far larger burden of childcare and home duties than a man, which impact her mental and physical health as well as job security. The way that an individual's identities overlap and reinforce each other is known as intersectionality.[1] Brianna also has a history of trauma, not just due to the racism she has experienced but also due to losing her father at a young age, but she does not have a family history of alcohol abuse.

In order to change our relationship with alcohol, we have to work to heal and manage the bottom layers of the iceberg. Some of the layers will never be resolved, and that is okay. While we can work through and heal trauma, we are changed by it. While we can manage our anxiety, depression, or other mental health disorder, we cannot eradicate it. And while we can fight for policy change that will provide equitable living situations for all, it is unlikely we will personally live to see the day without those systems. However, using the tools in this book, we can change our relationship with alcohol and create a life we don't need to escape from, and in turn, change our lives.

The Overlap of Diet Culture and Alcohol Culture

As you can probably guess, I tread lightly in my initial conversation with Brianna. She is feeling proud and excited, and while I try to highlight the importance of focusing on one thing at a time, she is excited about the possibility of changing her life and her body. After a few weeks of adhering to her rigid workout routine and diet, she comes into my office with a very different look on her face.

"Uh oh, what's that look on your face?" I ask.

"I don't know, Amanda, it's just not . . . working."

"Sobriety?"

"No. That's been fine. I didn't drink. Though I have wanted to if I am being honest." I nod. "I just feel like a failure. I've never struggled with food this much. Things were so good a few weeks ago. I was working out six days a week like she suggested, following through with the meal plan, feeling really healthy. I lost a few pounds. But now. . . . I'm off the rails. I have been binging on ice cream after my kids and husband go to bed. I'm so embarrassed . . . I wait for them to go to sleep so they don't see me." Tears start to stream down her face, but she is quick to brush them away. "I'm sorry," she says.

"Brianna," I say gently, "there is *nothing* wrong with you. This isn't a problem with you, this is the problem with diet culture."

Let me give you some backstory. Nutritionist Christy Harrison defines diet culture as "a system of beliefs that equates thinness, muscularity, and particular body shapes with health and moral virtue; promotes weight loss and body reshaping as a means of attaining higher status; demonizes certain food groups while elevating others; and oppresses people who don't match its supposed picture of health."[2] Diet culture is incredibly sneaky because it is a master shapeshifter. Most people in the twenty-first century understand that diets, in the strict sense of restricting your calorie intake, are ineffective and can lead to regaining the weight you lost, plus more over time. So now companies tout the need for "lifestyle changes." No longer do we see Atkins and Jenny Craig. We now are sold the health benefits of Noom, keto, paleo, and intermittent fasting. Heck, even Weight Watchers has gotten in on this trend and renamed itself as "*myWW+*" (because apparently the word "weight" is not good branding anymore).

The problem is most of these "lifestyle changes" are just diets in disguise. For example, Noom's tagline is "Stop dieting. Get lifelong results." However, Noom works by having participants log their food choices and giving them a calorie budget target of the day, with more calories allotted if you exercise. Noom's program is also filled with tips on how to reduce hunger, feel fuller, and promote mindful eating, but the program is essentially a calorie counting and reduction diet. Just as most diets, Noom does not offer information or statistics on the ability for its users to maintain long-term weight loss. The truth is, statically sound, long-term studies demonstrate that 90–95 percent of people who attempt to lose weight regain the weight they lost or regain more within five years.[3] As Christy Harrison states in her 2019 book *Anti-Diet*, "Even the most optimistic research shows that 'successful' participants will have maintained an average weight loss of just a few pounds after five years—and that's after gaining back more than 75 percent of the weight they initially lost."[4] Given this data, is it any wonder why diets have spent so much money over the past few decades completely rebranding themselves as lifestyle programs?

Now, I want to be clear, I am not against feeling better. I am not against eating in a way that fuels your body or feels good. I am not against exercise or movement. I am not against health. I am a huge believer that our mental health is very intertwined with our physical health. What I am against is a system that tells people—especially women, people in larger bodies, and people of color—that how they look is not good enough, and then profits off that insecurity. The diet industry is estimated to be worth $72 billion.[5] Furthermore, Western culture's fear and demonization of fat existed long before doctors could claim this was due to poor health outcomes. As sociologist Sabrina Strings discusses in her 2019 book, *Fearing the Black Body*, "The current anti-fat bias in the United States and in much of the West was not born in the medical field. Racial scientific literature since at least the eighteenth century has claimed that fatness was 'savage' and 'black.'"[6] Unfortunately, the science and medical field is not free from bias, and many studies over the past century have reinforced the belief that weight is equivalent to health, when the truth is that studies demonstrate that there are greater health risks with being underweight rather than overweight.[7] In fact, quite a few studies, including one by Lindo Bacon and Lucy Aphramor, indicate that excessive exercise and weight loss can cause higher levels of stress hormones and poorer health outcomes.[8] Instead, we need to recognize that weight does not equal health. And exercise and diet are only two factors that can improve our health. Let's not forget that sleep, sunlight, rest, going to regular doctor and dentist appointments, and limiting alcohol and drugs also affect our physical and mental health.

So why am I talking about this? After all, this is a book about alcohol, not eating disorders. The rate of overlap of eating disorders and substance use disorders is incredibly high, with some studies indicating up to 46 percent of individuals with an eating disorder also have a substance use disorder.[9] If you have a history of trauma, especially a diagnosis of PTSD, these statistics are even higher. Keep in mind these statistics only include individuals who actually fit both DSM-5 diagnoses, and most of these studies do not even include eating disorder diagnoses such as Atypical Anorexia, Orthorexia, or Eating Disorder Not Otherwise Specified (EDNOS). According to a CDC study done in 2018, half of Americans reported trying to lose weight in the past year.[10] So, there is a high probability that if you are reading this book (especially if you are a woman or nonbinary person), you have dieted, engaged in some kind of disordered eating, or have struggled with your body image in the past, or you will in the future and are therefore more at risk for developing an eating disorder or retriggering an old one when you stop drinking.

There are a few reasons why this happens. First, drinking and diet-ing are intertwined for a lot of us because many diets call for quitting drinking or limiting the type of alcohol or quantity that we consume (so we don't "waste" calories!). You may have memories of "breaking a diet" with drinking, so it is natural that when we stop drinking, we may also believe we need to restrict our eating in some way as well. Second, it's important to acknowledge that statistically speaking, when people stop drinking, they often feel hungrier, crave sugar (at least in the beginning), and can potentially gain weight. This is more likely if a lot of your calories have been coming from alcohol because your body is going to naturally want more food and nutrients.

You may also turn to food like ice cream in order to comfort your-self or deal with boredom, or you may eat an entire plate of chicken fingers to cope with the anxiety of being sober at a holiday party. (Been there!) You may even find yourself being more preoccupied with food, hoarding food, or feeling anxious if you don't have enough on hand. This does not mean that you are a food addict or a sugar addict! I can-not stress this enough. Your body is reacting appropriately to being deprived of food, whether that was on purpose (through restricting your food intake or purging to make up for calories in alcohol, aka "drunkorexia") or because you drank so much you didn't eat enough. I hear more and more people being afraid they are addicted to sugar or food, but the truth is that the studies on food and sugar addiction are incredibly flawed.

In 2016, a review of all the scientific studies on sugar addiction determined there was not enough evidence to support the theory that sugar is addictive.[11] To start, they are only done on animals, not humans. We would not only need human studies to prove this, but studies that are able to be repeated multiple times on large groups of people. Furthermore, as Christy Harrison states, "Only when the animals are periodically *deprived* of sugar do they eat in a way that might look or feel 'addictive.' The deprivation—not any chemical properties of food itself—drives their bingeing."[12] And the most crucial piece of data that is often overlooked in food addiction studies is the fact that putting people on diets that restrict their calories or limit the type of food they can eat causes people to crave that food more.˙ Food, unlike alcohol, is not an addictive substance. **Food is not a drug.** We need to consume it to survive. Abstaining from drugs or alcohol does not make you want them more—after you detox, if you are physically addicted—it makes you crave them *less*. Eventually, if you build a life that you do not need to escape from, you will truly not want alcohol at all. I promise.

Let's say this isn't your experience. You have no history of an eating disorder, and just want to build healthy habits that make you feel good. There's nothing wrong with that. However, my recommendation is to work on one thing at a time. The reasons are twofold. One—stopping drinking is hard enough as it is. If it wasn't, you probably wouldn't be spending your time reading this book. There is no need to make it harder by trying to change multiple things at once. Get a few months under your belt free from drinking, and then if you want to look into your health routines, great. I am not saying don't exercise or do other things that may help you cope with not drinking; I am simply saying take the pressure off and lower your expectations for yourself. Refrain from setting any other lofty goal other than staying sober. Two—when you stop drinking, all your feelings come rushing back. As Brianna demonstrates, it can feel alluring to overhaul your life. Dieting, restricting, or trying to change your body may allow you to feel powerful and in control of your life and your emotions during

---

* For more information, look into the Minnesota Starvation Experiments.

a time when you may feel scared and lost. However, going on a diet or "lifestyle change" in order to avoid dealing with the discomfort of sobriety is not going to allow you to develop the skills you need for success. Furthermore, as we discussed, the diet will be difficult to sustain long term. When this happens, you are likely to beat yourself up and give up on your new wellness routine, leading you to feel worse than when you started. If you feel really crappy, you may even say screw it all, and start drinking again.

Yes, a reason to quit drinking is that you may look and feel better, but it's important to recognize when your life starts to become a never-ending quest for perfection. You are a human, not a project. And the goal of sobriety is to live fully, not to put all the time, money, and energy you save from alcohol into diet culture. You are worthy and important regardless of your weight or how you look. You also do not *owe* your health to anyone. More and more in this day and age, we seem to equate health with morality, as though people are morally obligated to be healthy. I want to remind you, this is your life, and you get to choose how you live it. That can include engaging in diet culture if you want to. However, I want you to know the root of alcohol and diet culture are THE SAME! In 2019, the alcohol industry in the United States was estimated to be valued at $252 billion.[13] Both the diet and alcohol industries sell us the same idea: There is something wrong with us and they have the solution to fix us. Diet culture promises that if you just buy this diet product or don't eat this food, you will lose weight and feel happy, accepted, and have the life you want. Alcohol culture promises that if you buy and drink this beverage, you will feel happy, accepted, and have the life you want. The product may be different, but the promises are the same. If you aren't sure if this is something that affects you, here's a handy list to help you decide.

Signs You May Need to Heal Your
Relationship with Food or Exercise

- You often worry about what you just ate or what you are going to eat later
- You beat yourself up for eating dessert
- You have food rules. For example, you are only allowed to eat pizza on Fridays, you only allow yourself to eat cake on your birthday, or you do not allow yourself to eat anything with "added sugar"
- You cannot skip a day without exercising. If you do, you feel anxious or beat yourself up
- You spend a lot of time each day worrying about your food or weight
- You only engage in exercise that allows you to know how many calories you've burned
- You do not allow yourself to engage in movement like dance, yoga, stretching, or walking, or if you do, you do not count this as exercising
- You track calories, macros, or net carbs
- You have a history of being on and off diets
- If you gain weight, you do not allow yourself to buy new clothes (if you can afford them), instead you seek to lose weight
- You spend time in the mirror each day body checking (noting and touching your body to see if it has changed)
- The idea of not knowing how much you weigh gives you immense anxiety

Other Addictive Behaviors

"So, I think I may be addicted to . . . work. Is that a thing?" Tara asks me toward the end of our session.

"What do you think workaholism is?" I ask.

"But I don't have a fancy job. I don't care about being amazing at work. I just want to make a lot of money," Tara says with a laugh.

"That's actually more common than you think."

"Really?!" Tara asks genuinely.

"Yup, money can feel powerful."

"I get that, I have lost a lot of money gambling in the past."

"Yes, we can get addicted to anything that gives us a sense of control. Even if we know it's a false sense of control like gambling, where we know that we can't actually control the outcome," I explain.

"Yeah, but I *can* control how much I work. So, it just feels like real control."

"Right, but what are you actually controlling?" I ask. Tara and I had an entire session last week on the iceberg theory and how she used to use alcohol and sex to numb and suppress her emotions and trauma.

"Oh . . . my emotions. Okay, yes, fine, Amanda, I remember. At least this is a positive outlet, though right?!" Tara says cheekily.

"It is absolutely better than drinking or drugging or other things, Tara. It just is not actually effective at controlling your emotions or working through those deeper layers of the iceberg. But I also want to make sure you don't get so caught up in working and making money that you neglect your self-care and cause yourself so much stress that you are triggered to drink."

The illusion of being able to control our emotions is at the heart of almost any addictive behavior, whether that is alcohol, drug use, disordered eating, workaholism, gambling, shopping, and relationships. We get hooked by the idea that something else will fill us up or solve our problems. With all these behaviors, we feel as though we can change ourselves with this external thing. Just like alcohol ads promise us we will feel happy and carefree by drinking this beer and diet culture promises us we will be happy and popular if we buy their product and lose weight, workaholism promises us that if we are successful enough, we will finally be happy. Gambling promises us that if we make enough money, we will be happy. Shopping says if we buy the right clothes or have the right stuff, we will be fulfilled. And love addiction tells us that if we find the right relationship, we will finally feel complete. Remember the trap of innovation from Chapter 2? There's nothing wrong with you for feeling this way. The temptation to want more, to never be satisfied, to want solutions to how you are feeling is very *human*. The problem is that these behaviors do not actually help us feel better in the long term. They are not real self-care, and sometimes they can actually make us feel worse and cause more problems for us over time. However, it's important to work on the behavior that is causing you the most problems first. You don't need to work through everything at once. If you start noticing yourself falling into other addictive patterns, be compassionate and kind to yourself. Try to refrain from judging yourself. Process your emotions (Chapter 8) and practice real self-care (Chapter 9).

Chapter 12

Socializing While Sober

I relied on alcohol to loosen my tongue.
"Actually," I would say, leaning in after
the second glass, "I'm a wreck."
"I'm a wreck, too!" the woman would say, because
every female was hoarding some secret misery.

—Sarah Hepola

"I just miss who I was when I was drinking," Andrea says at the beginning of her session.

"What do you miss?" I ask.

"I miss being outgoing. I don't know what's wrong with me! I just feel like I need alcohol to be able to be social."

"Well, in fairness, Andrea, I think a lot of people might feel that way if they stopped drinking. Drinking is kind of like social lubricant."

"Yeah, but I'm just so shy. I hate it about myself."

"I unfortunately think a lot of people who are shy feel that way. Our society honestly tends to glamorize and prioritize people who are really outgoing. Most celebrities, prominent figures, influencers, all appear to be really outgoing."

"I guess so. I don't know. Ugh. I just wish sober socializing wasn't so damn hard!"

"You're right Andrea, it definitely can be challenging."

Why Sober Socializing Is So Hard

Much like Andrea, many people do not explore sobriety or go back to drinking after a period of time because they are afraid of the social repercussions. It's one of the most common reasons! We fear people will judge us; either they will think we are an alcoholic or a loser. We fear feeling different than other people, especially if we have a tendency toward shyness, get overwhelmed when meeting new people, or experience social anxiety. The truth is, many of us started drinking in high school, so we never learned how to actually meet new people, make friends, network, date, or socialize without a drink in hand, whether that's a legal beer at a bar or a swig of jungle juice from a red plastic cup. In fact, the most recent data from the CDC states that in 2019, 29 percent of high school students reported drinking alcohol, with 14 percent engaging in binge drinking.[1] A 2018 study by the National Survey on Drug Use and Health reported that 54.9 percent of full-time college students reported drinking in just the past month.[2] With so many people who start drinking regularly before their brains even finish developing (around age twenty-five), is it any wonder why so many of us are so heavily reliant on alcohol to socialize?

Another barrier to socializing sober is the fact that Western society tends to favor individuals who are outgoing and highly sociable, aka extroverts. Despite the fact that studies show that about 50 percent of our society is made up of introverts, modern life is generally set up in order to cater to extroverts. Parents worry about their children being shy, and our culture often encourages introverts to become more extroverted, as if all introverts' true and best selves are more outgoing. Susan Cain calls this concept the extrovert ideal, which she defines as the "omnipresent belief that the ideal self is gregarious, alpha, and comfortable in the spotlight." Cain tracks the rise of the extrovert ideal in her bestselling book *Quiet* with the rise of industrialization and urban living. Cain states, "Americans found themselves working no longer with neighbors but with strangers. 'Citizens' morphed into 'employees,' facing the question of how to make a good impression on people to whom they had no civic engagement with or family ties."[3] The answer to that problem came in the form of self-help. Self-help books switched from touting the importance of character and decency to advice on how to be confident, sell yourself, and have a winning personality.[4] Historian Warren Susman argues that America morphed from a Culture of Character to a Culture of Personality where "every American was to become a performing self." Advertisers were also quick to use this shift in order to sell their products, recognizing that if they tapped into people's fears and insecurities, they could sell more effectively. One advertisement for women's soap in 1922 warned, "All around you people are judging you silently. . . . Don't let little evidence of neglect—carelessness about your appearance—create an unfavorable impression."[5] Though advertisers may not be as obvious in their ads today, the underlying messages remain.

While everyday products such as soap, shaving cream, and clothes were sold as the cure to lack of confidence, no product was more successful in selling itself as the prescription to success than the cigarette. In fifty short years it went from making up only 2 percent of American tobacco consumption to 80 percent by 1952 . . . all because of advertising. One person who was instrumental to the cigarette's rise in popularity was Edward Bernays, a pioneer of the field of public relations and propaganda. Bernays was inspired by his uncle Sigmund

Freud's work, specifically about the group mind and how humans are influenced by irrational behavior.[6] He used this to invent the concept of engineering consent, which essentially is the process by which consumers are conned into believing that their choices around what they buy, wear, eat, drink, etc., are based solely on their own volition, when in fact, propaganda plays on our biologically hardwired desire to want to fit in. In Bernays's words, "If we understand the mechanisms and motives of the group mind, it is now possible to control and regiment the masses according to our will without their knowing it."[7] Bernays's ability to convince millions of women to smoke when it was taboo became his crowning achievement.

It wasn't long after big tobacco's success that big alcohol started using the same mechanisms to sell their own products, Holly Whitaker notes in her book *Quit Like a Woman*. She writes, "The alcohol industry didn't have to convince women that alcohol was the elixir of women's lib[eration] like the tobacco industry had to convince women that the cigarette was a Torch of Freedom; all they had to do was put a drink in her hand next to her cigarette."[8] As they fled their small towns in the twentieth century in hopes of making it in the big city, people became extremely fixated on having a good personality and making a good impression. With the rise of the cinema during this time, movie stars, who were always portrayed as being magnetic and outgoing, became cultural icons in America. Therefore, it is not a surprise that cigarettes and alcohol, which were put into the hands of movie stars, were easily sold as the cure for introversion, shyness, and lack of confidence. In 2022, we are still being sold alcohol as the solution to our problems. However, with the invention of social media, we sell alcohol to one another through Instagram, TikTok, and other influencer marketing hubs. Like cigarettes, people also seem to be waking up to the negative effects of alcohol, but time will tell whether that thinking will create a permanent shift and/or if another product or drug will fill the potential gap.

How to Tell People You Aren't Drinking

"I think it may be helpful to tell people you aren't drinking right now," I say to Andrea next week when she reveals that she hasn't told anyone besides her fiancé. This has led to her completely avoiding social outings for the past two months.

"I don't want to them to judge me."

"I understand that. What makes you think they will judge you?"

"I just feel like it's what people in my class do. Work hard, play hard. All of our social activities with med school are set up around drinking or at a bar. It's weird for someone my age to just not drink. I already struggle with feeling shy and feeling like I don't fit in. I don't want to draw any more attention to myself."

"It can definitely feel scary. But I also don't think this is sustainable if you want to stop drinking. You don't have to go to a bar or spend time with those people if you feel uncomfortable, but I don't think isolating yourself from everyone is good for your mental health."

"I know. You're right. It's not even about the drinking or being triggered at a bar. I want to spend time with my classmates. I'm not worried about that. I just . . . I don't have the words. What do I say?"

"You say . . . I'm not drinking tonight."

"But what if they ask why?"

Andrea has a fair point. Almost every time someone indicates that they aren't drinking, the most common follow-up question is why. As comedian Jim Gaffigan says in a stand-up routine, "When you don't drink, people always need to know why. This never happens with anything else. [They're never like] 'You don't use mayonnaise—why?!'" So, in regard to answering this question that you will unfortunately and undoubtedly be asked, I have four words for you: DON'T USE AN EXCUSE. While it may be tempting to say things such as "I am the designated driver tonight" or "I have to get up early tomorrow because I'm moving," try not to blame your lack of drinking on something external. Because in my personal and professional experience, it is amazing the lengths people will go to solve the problem called "not drinking tonight." The most selfish people will all of a sudden offer to pay for your and everyone else's Ubers home or help you move in the morning, if given the opportunity. And once they do that, you are going to be in a very awkward position of having to turn down the most generous offer someone has ever made you. Instead, keep it simple and generic. Say you are taking a break from drinking. Say you are not drinking for health reasons. Say you just aren't feeling it tonight. Remember the boundaries chapter, you have a right to say no without providing an explanation why.

At a certain point, if you decide you are interested in continuing this sober experiment for the long haul, it may be helpful to tell people you are close to that you are no longer drinking. Or if you are meeting people you know you will see again, such as people at work, telling people you don't drink is easier than having to tell them you aren't drinking tonight every time you see them. It may take more work to do, there may be more questions, but it is a way of saving yourself time and energy in the future, if you feel as though you are able to do it. Here are a few things you can say . . .

- "I've drunk enough for a lifetime."
- "I choose not to."
- "I assure you, I have a very good reason [*wink*]."
- "I feel better when I don't."
- "I'm in recovery/sober/an alcoholic [whatever word you like]."
- "I don't like the person I am when I drink."
- "It was preventing me from accomplishing my goals."

- "I hate having hangovers."
- "It doesn't mix well with my life."
- "I'm on medication." I am not the biggest fan of this one because people may ask you what medication and offer you an alternative med that will let you drink!
- "Because when I drink even a small amount, I feel terrible."
- "I'm focusing on my health right now."
- "I just don't like it."
- You could share some of your personal reasons.

How to Find Yourself and Your People

"Okay, I get that, but, Amanda, I have no hobbies. I've never had any hobbies. I've been drinking since I was twelve years old," Tara tells me.

"Is there anything you enjoy doing?" I ask.

"I like going to the bar!" Tara says in a deadpan way. I nod and pause so she will continue. "I don't know . . . " she says, gazing off. "I don't really know myself."

"Well, that's a good start." Tara gives me a look of confusion. I clear my throat. "I mean if you recognize that you don't *know* yourself, this is a good jumping-off point. Now we can start the process of getting curious and getting to know yourself."

"Okay, how?"

"Well, what did you like to do as a kid?"

"I told you, I've never had any hobbies."

"I know, but I mean think about being really young. It doesn't need to have been a hobby. What types of games did you play as a child? Did you like playing with other kids or alone? Did you prefer art class or gym in grade school?"

"Well, I used to really enjoy art class. But I'm not good at it."

"Exploring things that you are interested in is not about being good at it. It's about reconnecting with yourself. You are definitely creative on some level, Tara, or you wouldn't be interested in experimenting with your hair colors." Tara's hair is a purple color this week. "I also would try doing some regular things and see if you enjoy them. You may have a different level of enjoyment from doing simple things like doing a puzzle or thrifting, for example, now that you are sober. You may be surprised at what you like now that your brain doesn't have such a skewed tolerance for pleasure due to your alcohol and drug consumption." Tara nods. "And if you start doing things that you enjoy, you will be more likely to find people who have similar interests to yours."

"Yeah, I guess you're right. My only real friends right now are people I've met in rehabs or at work because that's all I've really done in the past few years since high school."

"Exactly," I say. "Having friends that are sober is great, and I am all about you doing that. But I also think it can be great to tap into other types of friendships. You are a complex, unique human, whose identity can be more than 'doesn't drink alcohol.'" Tara laughs.

"Okay so let's say I . . . I don't know, join an art class or something . . . how do I take that beyond just talking to them in art class? It's not like dating where there is an end goal. Friendship is so . . . murky."

"That's true. But I also think a lot of the same principles apply. Think about how you made friends when you were young. My guess is you probably met people in school and had playdates with them. Your parents may have set that up, but that's how you made friends."

"So, what, just ask them to coffee?"

"Yup!"

Exercise: Grab a journal and a piece of paper. Answer the following questions.

1. What did I used to love to do as a child?
2. Did I gravitate more toward art, gym, or music class?

3. What do I like to do that doesn't involve alcohol?
4. Have I ever had moments of being so immersed in something I lost sense of time? What was I doing?

Whether you relate more to Andrea's experience of feeling shy and not knowing how to tell people you aren't drinking, or if you relate more to Tara and feel like the only interest you have ever had is bar hopping, it's important to take time to get to know yourself in sobriety. Many people are surprised to learn what they enjoy doing and what isn't fun anymore without alcohol to smooth everything over. We convince ourselves that alcohol is what makes us and others fun and interesting, but what if we only need alcohol because we don't actually like what we are doing or who we are spending time with? Ask yourself . . . do I really like going to a super-crowded bar that reeks of beer, while people talk over one another? Do I like going to sports games and hanging out in a parking lot for a few hours before? Do I enjoy spending time with friends when I don't have drunken nights or interesting cocktails to bond over? None of these questions have right or wrong answers, but they are important questions to unpack for yourself. Maybe you do truly enjoy going to a crowded bar, and having a beer is just a cherry on top of the experience. If that's true, then I encourage you to do that sober to make sure you truly enjoy it and so you can learn to do it without the booze. It is only once we learn how to do something sober that we can then choose freely if we want to drink in that situation. Otherwise, we may be drinking in order to have fun or to cope with anxiety, fear, or awkwardness.

Getting sober is like getting glasses for the first time. If you have ever had the experience, you may recall the feeling of realizing how blurry your vision was. There is a big, wide, colorful, and clear world that has always existed, and you had no idea it was possible! Without alcohol, everything becomes clearer. While this can be really exciting because you may start to get more joy out of simple things, it may be a rude awakening to realize your friendships, relationships, job, or hobbies may not be very fulfilling. You may realize you have social anxiety and you have been using alcohol as a crutch. This can be a scary feeling, and one that can unfortunately lead people back to drinking. However, it's important to remember that continuing to drink in an effort to avoid facing yourself will not lead to a meaningful and fulfilling life, but one where you are dependent on alcohol in order to cope.

Remember to take one thing at a time and know that you don't have to change anything you don't want to. Getting sober is about getting to know your true self and building a life you don't want to escape from, not Marie Kondo–ing your entire life. Sobriety doesn't mean it will be free from pain, or that every aspect of your life will bring you joy. Reparenting yourself is not always fun, but it will dramatically support you in living a purposeful and value-driven life. Life is always going to be filled with difficulties, but a sober life means you will have the capacity and the tools (refer back to part 2!) to deal with it honestly and head on.

Exercise: Make a list of things you enjoyed doing when drinking and do them sober. Notice if you actually enjoy doing them or if they are not tolerable or fun without a drink in your hand. If you are unsure about why certain things are enjoyable, get specific. For example, I still enjoy going to bars if they are not too crowded, and if they have great ambiance and design. However, going to a dive bar isn't worth it or fun for me. I also have a higher tolerance for going to bars where they offer mocktails or kombucha, or if there is an activity to do such as pool or skee-ball. Some things though, like wine tasting, are never worth it for me. No matter how beautiful the scenery and ambiance are, I feel way too uncomfortable when I go. I will never go to a sports game because I truly have zero interest. I avoid networking events at all costs but do enjoy going to classes or events where there is something to do and socializing and drinking are not the only focus. Get curious and note your tolerance may change over time and depend on whom you are with. As an introvert, I have a higher tolerance for being around alcohol if I am fully recharged and have been taking care of myself versus if I am feeling stressed and burned out.

Making Friends as an Adult

So, you may be thinking, this is great info, but how do I actually *make* friends as an adult? Great question. Let's dive into the three different types of friendships.

Utility Friendships—these are the types of friendships where your connection with each other is based on usefulness. Think about work friends, business partners, classmates, neighbors, maybe someone who's in your same field whom you swap advice with. Maybe this person is close to your close friends, so you are friends with them simply because you see them often. These friendships are typically not someone you would necessarily pick to be friends with, but the friendship is mutually beneficial for both parties. Since these friendships are not based on companionship, they tend to be short-lived, and these friendships do not endure if you no longer see each other.

Pleasure Friendships—these are the types of friendships where your connection is based on enjoyment of each other. This could be because you find each other really funny, you enjoy the types of conversations you have, or you have similar hobbies. While these friendships are typically deeper than utility friendships, these types of friends and your closeness to them can also change over time as your idea of fun and pleasure changes as well.

Close Friendships—these are the types of friendships most of us crave. While these people could have started as friendships of utility or pleasure, they are people with whom we develop deep connections. Close friendships are based on mutual love and care for each other, honesty, and reciprocity. These friendships can be a best friend situation where you talk and see each other a lot, or they can also be the type where you don't often see or talk to each other, but when you do it is as if no time has passed between you.

As you examine your relationship with alcohol, you may recognize that some of your friendships are utility friends and are not pleasurable to spend time around when you remove alcohol from the equation. This is a normal process to go through. You may also realize that some of your other friendships grow stronger when you recognize you have more in common now that you want to spend time doing activities with them beyond drinking. You may also recognize that you are in need of sober friends or people who really "get it." I would say almost everyone needs at least one sober friend to confide in. In this case, you may want to try recovery meetings, Instagram groups, sober bars, or meetups. You may also try ditching your anonymity and being open about your sobriety, as this will make it easier for you to identify others who also do not drink.

One common pattern I see in my work with clients is that people often put a lot of pressure on their friendships. We can get caught in the trap of wanting no friendships of utility and pleasure and just wanting close friendships. However, it's important to remember that not everyone will be able to meet our needs. You are a multifaceted human being and as a result benefit from a healthy mix of people who can support

your different preferences, interests, hobbies, and environment. Having a healthy mix of friendships of utility, pleasure, and closeness is best for your mental health. The suggestions above may spark some ideas for you for finding various types of friends you may need or want.

I'm not going to lie, like all things in sobriety, it *is* going to take more work and effort to socialize and make friends without alcohol. However, in my personal and professional experience, if you stick with it and learn the skills that you didn't develop while you were drinking, the end result will be more authentic and deep connections. As Catherine Gray says in her memoir *The Unexpected Joy of Being Sober*, "Drunk bonding is like a glue stick. It's cheap and it sticks quickly. But it's also easily torn asunder. Whereas sober bonding is more like cement. It takes a heckofalot longer to set."[9]

Without the haze of alcohol, we know ourselves better and therefore know what we want and need in a friend, and we can more clearly see people for who they are. If you are looking to create more close friendships, look for these eight qualities.

It's normal for these qualities to ebb and flow. Try not to expect a perfect 50/50 split in the relationship. Let's face it, some of us are better at planning or remembering to reach out than others, but as long as this is communicated and the friendship works for both of you, it is likely worth keeping. And when conflict arises, as it always will, go back to Chapter 10 and remember the importance of setting boundaries.

Ideas for Where to Meet Friends IRL:

- Yoga or exercise studios
- Personal development workshops
- Art or dance classes
- Hiking or running clubs. Sometimes these are even organized by running or sports clothing stores such as Lululemon.
- Networking events
- Book clubs

- Sober bars (Sober bars are popping up more and more around the country, especially if you live in a major city. Check out the resources section for specifics!)
- Daybreaker (a morning dance party in cities across the United States)
- Volunteer opportunities. What causes are you passionate about? See if there are local organizations you can get involved with in your area.
- Twelve-step and/or recovery-based meetings (AA, NA, Al-anon, SMART, Y12SR [Yoga of 12 Step Recovery], Refuge Recovery)

Ideas for Finding Friends Online:

- Use meetup.com where you can search by activity and local events
- Get to know your neighbors using the Nextdoor app
- Use Instagram or other social media. Join groups and follow pages and hashtags with similar interests—there are lots of sober groups and pages—and chat up a conversation with someone you respect and see if they are interested in grabbing coffee
- Use a friend-finding app: Athleto, Bumble BFF, CLIQ, Friend-match, Peanut, Meet My Dog, RealU, Skout, etc.

Chapter 13

Love, Sex, and Romance

I love a martini—but two at the most. Three I'm
under the table, four, I'm under the host.

—Dorothy Parker

"So, I am pretty sure I am going to be single forever," Tara says.

I smile. "Oh yeah?"

"Yup, this is the longest I have ever been sober and honestly the idea of going out on a date . . . like dating is straight up not meant for sober people. Alcohol is required."

"Okay, what about your friends, have they dated since getting sober?"

"Well, a lot of my friends are lucky and have significant others already. Or they are just on tons of dating apps. And I don't know, I just don't feel comfortable telling people I don't drink before I've even met them. It's too much!"

"I get that, it can definitely be overwhelming," I say.

"So, it's settled, I am going to be single forever then!" Tara says in her half joking, self-deprecating way.

"Tara . . . " I say, joking back.

"No, it's fine, I will get another cat or two. I will just be the fun single friend forever. Except not really fun because I don't drink. So I will just settle for being the crazy cat lady, I guess."

Tara's beliefs about sober dating are extremely common. Sober dating is like sober socializing on steroids. Not only are you meeting a new person, having to talk to them in an intimate setting, but there is also the possibility of sexual intimacy. Oh yes, and let's not forget that the person is also likely to recommend that you go out for a drink, which puts your drinking or lack thereof front and center and will probably make you *really* want to drink to ease the awkwardness. However, the beauty of sober dating is that you are able to see the person for who they are much more clearly without the haze of alcohol clouding your vision. It may be more uncomfortable, especially in the beginning when you are getting used to it, but overall, I find that people who don't drink alcohol on dates are able to save a lot of time and energy because they know if someone is a match for them more quickly. Like all things in sobriety, it's more difficult at first, but whether you want to date in search of a relationship or are interested in a hookup, it will lead to you finding a more genuine connection.

Let's break down what this looks like. You can learn a lot about someone simply by how they react when you say you don't drink. This may happen before you meet up in person. Some people choose to put it on their profile if they are online dating. There is also an opportune time to disclose this if the person suggests getting a drink as the first date. It could also happen during the date when you decline a drink from the waiter and order a different beverage. If the person makes fun of you, tries to pressure you into drinking, calls you a name, degrades you in any capacity, or justifies and makes comments about their own drinking, these are all red flags that you got to discover about them *early.* On the other hand, if they are unbothered, curious, understanding, or, dare I say, respect you and your decision, these are undoubtedly green flags, both of which you get to discover very quickly.

While it is completely up to you whether you disclose you don't drink on your profile or before you meet up in person, one thing I would discourage you from doing is lying about the fact that you don't drink. Not only have I heard horror stories about clients accidentally drinking because they weren't honest and arrived at the bar early to orchestrate the bartender serving them a seltzer and lime ("But make it look like a vodka soda!"), but using an excuse with your date is likely to backfire or result in you having to admit to lying, a red flag for your date. Instead, I would recommend saying something along the lines of "I'm not drinking right now" or "I'm taking a break from drinking." This is honest, but also gives you space to continue on your sobriety journey if you wish without lying. It also tells your date that you would probably appreciate doing something else besides going to a bar if another date happens in the future.

It's good to know that the first fifteen minutes of a date (or any social gathering at a restaurant or bar) is the most difficult. It is during those first fifteen minutes that people eagerly order a drink, and you may feel awkward. This is when people might ask why you aren't drinking. Remember to draw on the list of responses from the last chapter. But, once they settle in with their drink, the energy shifts and it's easier to connect with them.

Finally, I would be remiss if I didn't mention the other advantage to dating sober. You are more likely to stick to your values and not do something you regret. My guess is if you are reading this book, you hooked up with someone when you were drunk that you never would have sober, whether this is kissing someone or having sex. You have also probably said or done something you regret or divulged some things about yourself that were not appropriate for a first date because your prefrontal cortex—the rational, decision-making part of your brain—was asleep. You will be able to date more confidently knowing that you are living a life that is in alignment with what you want, need, and value in a relationship.

Modern dating culture glorifies drinking as a way to "loosen up" and be more comfortable. Alcohol does reduce our inhibitions, but inhibitions serve a purpose. An inhibition is "a voluntary or involuntary restraint on the direct expression of an instinct."[1] Your instincts keep you safe. They say, "I can't quite put my finger on it, but I'm getting a weird vibe from that guy." Your instincts say, "Yes, I feel really comfortable with them, but I don't feel ready to share that or do that." Your instincts are your bullshit meter. Your instincts remind you that you can set boundaries and remind you of the long-term consequences of the decisions you are going to make. Once you realize this, it may be easier than you think to trade the initial discomfort of not drinking for actually taking action that will get you closer to the life you want.

Managing Your Current Relationship

"Amanda, I don't know how to say this . . . I just feel like my sobriety is hurting my marriage." Brianna sits down on my couch, sounding desolate.

"Tell me what's going on," I say.

"We just keep getting into fights when he's drinking. I never cared before if he drank around me, but now that I've been sober for a few months, his drinking bothers me more."

"Any idea what changed?" I ask.

"Well, I think that I used to not notice or care. Like when I was sober for that period of time after I had Mia, I wasn't really sober on

Date Ideas That
Don't Involve Alcohol

- Go out for dessert
- Grab coffee
- Ice skating
- Bowling
- Comedy show
- Live music
- Go to a concert
- BYOB restaurant
- Workout class
- Go for a hike
- Volunteer
- Farmer's or flea market
- Amusement park
- Go to a sports game
- Go to an arcade
- Mini golfing
- Axe throwing
- Ping pong
- Go to a trivia night
- Take a class (art, cooking, crafting, etc.)
- Visit a museum
- Go to the movies
- Rock climbing
- Have a game night
- Go out dancing
- Have a picnic
- Take a walk
- Go to the beach

purpose. I was pregnant and didn't start drinking again because I was overwhelmed with the baby. Now, I am actually really enjoying being sober and I'm annoyed when my husband drinks."

"So, it sounds like before you didn't pay as much attention to whether he was drinking or not before because you weren't trying to not drink."

"Yeah. But now, I can see how he changes when he drinks. Like he isn't a different person, but he's just not. . . . present. He's not himself. I don't know how to describe it."

"I know what you mean," I say, and I do. My husband drinks and it annoys me when I can tell he isn't *fully there*. It's a really common stumbling block for people that get sober if they have a partner who does drink. The relationship can change, and it can be a scary thing to work through. However, even for sober folks who choose to be with a partner that drinks (I met my husband when I was two years sober), it can still come with disagreements. I ask, "What do you think it is about him not being present that bothers you?"

Brianna looks out the window thinking about my question. "I just feel like he's not with me. Like we have such little alone time together with how busy we are and the two kids. We go on a date once a month . . . if that. And when we do, I really want to be fully connected to him. But for him, we never get to go on a date, so he really wants to enjoy being at a restaurant by getting a drink. . . . Who's right in this situation?"

"I think you are both right. I understand why you both feel the way you do. Have you honestly told him how you feel?"

Brianna thinks for a moment and a smile spreads across her face. "No, I think I just get annoyed and start to nag him," she says with a laugh.

"I think you need to sit down and explain to him how you feel. Share your feelings, tell him what you told me rather than focusing on his drinking. Share that you miss him and want to feel connected to him and it's hard when he has had a drink. I think if he knew that, then he may be inclined to compromise."

What If My Partner Drinks?

If you are in a relationship with someone who drinks, once you start experiencing the positive benefits of sobriety, you may want your partner to stop drinking so they can experience the magic of sobriety too. Or you may start to notice how they use alcohol to numb out, de-stress, or deal with their emotions and you may want to point out that alcohol isn't actually helping them. Maybe you think your significant other drinks too much and are worried. It may be frustrating when you wake up sparkling and ready to go on Sunday morning and they have a hangover and don't want to leave the couch. And let's be honest, sober sex is great, but not when the other person is drunk. If you relate to any of these things, my advice is to honestly tell your significant other how you feel. **Do not make them wrong for drinking** (after all, you are the one that made the change), but do share how you feel. You have a right to set boundaries, but remember boundaries are about taking care of yourself, not changing another person.

Any change that happens to one partner in a relationship is going to change the dynamic of the relationship. Humans naturally resist change. Remember, this isn't personal. I've had spouses beg me to help their significant other quit drinking only to have them push back when their newly sober spouse starts setting boundaries that they don't like. A relationship unit—two people or more—wants to maintain status quo, and people may unconsciously push back on your sobriety in order to do so. This doesn't mean that your relationship is doomed. It *does* mean that you may need to help them understand that this is something you are doing for yourself and that you are not trying to change them. It also may be helpful to share how *they* will actually benefit from you being sober. For example, you may get into less drunken disagreements, they won't have to worry about your physical health or you putting yourself in harm's way, or they won't have to take care of you at 3 a.m.

Once your partner is supportive or accepting of your sobriety, know that you have a right to set boundaries **and** you may have to negotiate some boundaries in order to get both of your needs met. For example, you may want to set the boundary that you don't keep alcohol in your home. However, if you live with your partner, this may not be possible. In this case, maybe they can only buy alcohol that they are going to consume that week so there isn't an excess left around the house. There may be certain activities you opt out of doing with your partner that they are free to do with others. Or, in Brianna's case, aim to have two date nights a month, one that is alcohol free and the other that is at a place her husband chooses. The absolute best chance you have of convincing your partner to quit drinking alongside you is through inspiring them rather than trying to force them to change. AA has a slogan that stresses attraction over promotion, and I couldn't agree more.

While this may feel like a bummer to read, I want to remind you that every relationship has its challenges and compromises. Someone gets a new job; one person gets really into exercise; another person becomes a vegan; you have kids. Life is complicated and being in a committed partnership is not easy. There will always be stressors, but it is absolutely possible to be in a relationship where one person drinks and the other does not. Two sober folks dating each other can also come

Why It's Hard for One Person in the Relationship to Change

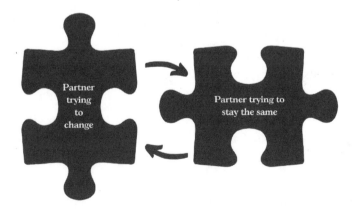

One partner's growth pushes against and impacts the other partner,
as well as the status quo of the relationship.

with stressors: relapse, worrying about the other slipping, being overly dependent on each other to stay sober. No relationship is perfect. You get to decide what works for you.

Sober Sex

"I've literally never had sex without drinking," Tara says toward the end of the session. I'm surprised by the fact that she isn't being self-deprecating.

I smile. "This is actually pretty normal."

Why is this? Well, our culture and alcohol companies suggest that alcohol is an aphrodisiac and makes you feel sexy. But, if we dig into what is *actually* happening when we drink, the truth is that alcohol just shuts off the part of the brain that makes you feel self-conscious. You are not actually more attractive, funnier, or better in bed, you just *feel* more confident because you aren't as concerned about how others are perceiving you. If you have ever been sober and seen how a drunk person acts during or before sex, you know what I mean. Being sloppy isn't sexy. Thinking you're going to puke isn't sexy. Slurring your words isn't sexy. And the belief that people are more attractive when you are drinking (aka beer goggles) is a myth that has been discredited.[2] This is an important distinction because for many of us, alcohol is so intertwined with sex and dating that we can feel it is impossible to get into the mood without it.

You also aren't actually more adventurous in bed, as in, you are more confident in knowing what you want; your inhibitions are just lowered. So, you are more likely to say yes to something while drunk that you wouldn't want to do if you were sober. While this can lead to a wider range of experiences, it's not actually helping you get in touch with and own your desires. And if you have a partner, your sexual intimacy and comfort with each other is not going to increase if you can only engage or talk about certain sexual acts and desires while you are under the influence.

Alcohol also doesn't make sex *feel better*. At all. Alcohol literally dulls nerve endings that allow you to experience sensation, which results in sex feeling less pleasurable. In men, alcohol also makes it more difficult to get an erection, and women are less likely to be lubricated. Alcohol makes it difficult for women to have orgasms, and those that are had are less intense.[3] And I'm not just talking about alcohol diluting the feeling during sex, I'm talking about foreplay and all the intimacy that can lead up to it. Have you ever been so incredibly aroused by someone stroking the side of your face? Holding your hand? Have you experienced the goose bumps that come with someone (the right person, mind you) gently whispering in your ear? Or experienced the intense butterflies of someone staring into your eyes, from across the room or on your doorstep as you wonder if you will kiss? These are all things that alcohol completely dulls the sensation of. While you may not feel the nervous butterflies of a first date, you also won't get to experience the excitement butterflies of a first kiss. In our hyperactive world of social media, technology, and better, faster, more, I think it's important to savor the tiny moments that remind me that I am alive.

Healing Your Relationship with Pleasure

A few weeks later, Tara and I meet for another session and she updates me on her dating and sex life. She says, "So there are a few things I need to say, and I need to say them right now so that I don't lose the courage to bring them up later." I nod intently. "I don't think I'm straight, but I don't know if I am gay or bi or queer or what. I don't know. We had sex. It was terrible. I faked it. Which isn't that abnormal, but I just never really realized I guess how uninterested I am in sex with men."

Intoxicated Sex Pros	Intoxicated Sex Cons
- Reduces self-consciousness so you may feel more confident - Reduces inhibitions and fear so you may be more willing to try new things - Can increase arousal initially	- Consent might be blurry - More difficult to orgasm/reach climax - More difficult to become aroused (men - getting hard; women - being lubricated) - You or partner may say or do things you regret - Can be sloppy - Harder to know what you want or need during sex - Less pleasure and reduced orgasm intensity as alcohol fills sensation - Reduced inhibitions may have you say yes to things you aren't comfortable with - More likely to engage in risky behavior (e.g.,not using protection) - Impedes true intimacy - Less likely to discover what you actually like sexually

"Did you want to have sex with him? Do you like him?" I ask.

"I don't know," she says, pausing to think. "Honestly, Amanda, I don't think I even asked myself this question. Like we went on a date, and he was nice enough, and I knew he wanted to have sex with me, so I just did. Never did I think to ask myself if I wanted to."

"I think that makes sense, Tara." I'm trying to help her break down her shame by normalizing this. "If you've never had sex when you were sober, you probably haven't had a lot of awareness to check in with yourself."

"Yeah, I guess. But honestly it's been getting me thinking . . . all the sex I've had . . . have I wanted any of it?" Tara looks out the window and I wait as she appears to collect her thoughts. She continues, "You know, the first time I had sex I was twelve years old. I was at a high school party and me and my friend Sarah lied and said we went to a different high school, so they all thought we were seventeen. I was proud of having sex with him in the bathroom because I wanted to get invited to more parties. I wanted to know high school kids who could get us beer."

"You learned how to use your body at a young age," I say.

"Yeah, because I'm a selfish alcoholic," Tara scoffs.

"Or maybe, you were trying to survive in the way you knew how."

"I just can't believe I never realized how inexperienced I am. Like I've had so much sex but never been present for it. How have I never even thought about what I wanted?"

"Well, I think a lot of women are taught that sex is for pleasing a man. I mean, think about it, where did you first learn about sex?"

"Guys I've been with . . . and porn." Tara looks up at me and looks embarrassed.

"Right, and let's be honest, most men get all their information from porn. And most of the porn industry is funded by and specifically created for men, so it focuses almost exclusively on male sexual pleasure." Tara nods and I ask, "What is your relationship with self-pleasure?"

"I mean I have done it before, but I don't really do it much . . . it just makes me . . . uncomfortable."

"Do you remember the first time you learned about it, or did it?"

"Well, it's weird because I had sex before I ever masturbated. So I liked to pretend to my friends that I orgasmed during sex and I was really experienced . . . and I was with sex, but I had no idea about masturbation or what to do."

"Tara, I think it may be helpful for you to work on healing your relationship with pleasure."

"What do you mean?"

"I mean, a lot of us have shame about pleasure. Whether this is because of our parents' reaction if they caught us masturbating, shame around having too much or not enough sex, sexual trauma, or from internalizing the belief in our culture that women who enjoy sex are slutty. Many of us never get proper sex education and are not even aware of or familiar with our own bodies."

"So, me hating sex with that guy doesn't mean I'm gay?"

"I don't know what it means. But I do think you starting to explore your sexuality, body, and relationship with pleasure is going to give you clarity."

Regardless if you relate to Tara's experience of questioning her sexuality, getting sober and starting to think about having sex can bring up a lot of emotions and memories. The most common experiences I hear women tell me when they get sober include

- Questioning their sexuality
- Working through shame around sex, whether this is because they have had too many or not enough sexual experiences
- Reckoning with the fact that they have been faking orgasms for most of their life. Maybe they've never had one, or they want to learn how to communicate this to a sexual partner.
- Learning how to masturbate and please themselves if they desire
- Learning how to honestly communicate what they like and don't like in bed
- Working through memories of sexual trauma or assault

- Recognizing how they have used sex as a way to numb their emotions or control others' behavior
- Working through body-image shame

Exercise: Grab a journal and a pen and write down the answers to the following questions.

1. What do you think about when you hear the word "pleasure"?
2. How did you first learn about sex? What beliefs does your family have about sex that may influence your own attitudes about it?
3. How did you first learn about masturbation and self-pleasure? How has this shaped your relationship with it?
4. Think about your best experiences and worst experiences with sex and identify what made them positive or negative.
5. How may you ask for what you want in the future or set boundaries around what you don't want? What do you want or like in sex that you don't ask for?

Body Image

When women in particular start engaging in sober sex, one of the most common things that they struggle with is their body image. While anyone can have difficulty getting aroused if they feel insecure about their body, women often struggle with this more than men. This is because, from an early age, women learn to objectify themselves. According to body image researchers Lindsay and Lexie Kite, "Self-objectification occurs when people learn to view their own bodies from an outside perspective, which is a natural result of living in an environment where bodies are objectified."[4] This results in us constantly monitoring our bodies and imagining how they look from an outside perspective. If you have ever had the experience of constantly tugging on your clothes to make sure they are laying just flat out of fear someone may perceive you as heavier, checking how your body looks at various angles in the mirror, or constantly imagining what someone may think of your body, even if you are alone, you know what I'm talking about. This is self-objectification. It's the voice in your head that is constantly monitoring how you look. It takes up a huge amount of time and energy and it is a huge buzzkill when it comes to getting in the mood to have sex.

Why is this? In *Come as You Are*, Emily Nagoski talks about something called the dual control model of sexual response, which explains how and why individuals get turned on and off. We have two models that work together: the Sexual Excitation System (SES), which is an "accelerator" of your sexual interest; and the Sexual Inhibition System (SIS), which is the "brake." According to Nagoski, "Just as the accelerator scans the environment for turn-ons, the brake scans for anything your brain interprets as a good reason not to be aroused right now— risk of STI transmission, unwanted pregnancy, social consequences etc."[5] In order to understand how easily or not easily someone can get aroused, we have to determine how sensitive their brakes and accelerator are. For example, someone with a higher sex drive will have a very sensitive accelerator and not sensitive brake (lots of things can turn them on and very few things can turn them off) while someone with a lower sex drive will not have a sensitive accelerator and have a very sensitive brake (it takes a lot to get turned on, and they are easily turned off). Understanding your unique sex drive is extremely helpful in reclaiming your relationship with pleasure and sex. Check the back of *Come as You Are* or google "Sexual Excitation System" to get the inventory to understand where you fall on the scale.

It probably won't come as a surprise to you that research says men tend to have more sensitive sexual accelerators, while women tend to have more sensitive brakes.[6] Some of the most common things that turn women off are insecurities about their body, concerns about their reputation or other's perception of them, and feeling used by a partner. Therefore, women struggle more than men to get sexually aroused because they more closely monitor how their body looks and their reputation (aka self-objectification) and worry about being used (aka being objectified). Alcohol inhibits the part of the brain that monitors our body and reputation and self-objectifies. It turns off the part of our brain that criticizes how we look. If we have internalized shame around sex, we can temporarily quit worrying if we will be slut-shamed later as alcohol makes us forget about potential repercussions of our actions. If we have a history of trauma and struggle to feel safe enough to be in our body, alcohol numbs our hypervigilance and the part of our brain that questions if we trust our partner or our own bodies. Therefore, alcohol isn't actually an aphrodisiac, it simply **makes your sexual brakes less sensitive**, making it easier for you to get sexually aroused.

So How Do We Start Taking Steps to Heal Our Relationship with Our Body Image?

- **Set boundaries.** You have a right to tell someone that you do not want them commenting on your body. You have a right to decide what someone is allowed to say or do. Refer back to Chapter 10 for the format of exactly *how* to set boundaries.
- **Aim for body neutrality** and focus on the things your body allows you to do instead of focusing on how it looks. You don't need to love your body in order to appreciate it or take care of it.
- **Break up with diet culture.** Stop trying to change your body. Often, we use our bodies as scapegoats for deeper feelings. We blame our bodies for feeling depressed, anxious, or angry so that we don't have to deal with how we are actually feeling. Loving

your body doesn't actually make you happy; all it does is take away one problem your brain wants to solve. Also, if you get the body you want, all you will do is find another body part or thing that needs to be fixed.

- **Stop waiting for your body to change.** Buy clothes that fit your body now (thrift or see if people have clothes who can donate to you if you cannot afford new ones). Your body deserves to be taken care of now, as it is.

- **Grieve the body you want.** Allow yourself to go through the process of denial, anger, depression, bargaining, and acceptance.

- **Practice self-compassion.** Talk to yourself the way you would talk to a friend. Remember that you are not alone in your struggles with body image. Practice mindfulness and remember *you are not your thoughts.* You *have* thoughts.

- **Expose yourself to different types of people and bodies.** Follow people on social media who look different than what you commonly see (white, cis, hetero, thin folks). Follow Black and brown folks, fat folks, people with disabilities, LGBTQ+ folks, people wearing hijabs, people wearing just their underwear. Let yourself view all different types of bodies.

- **Practice mindfully being in your body.** You can do this through gentle movement (walking, stretching, yoga), doing an activity that requires being in your body (washing dishes, cleaning, organizing), or through other sensations like taking a bath or shower, massage, body work, or acupuncture. Check back to Chapter 9 for more ideas on exactly how to engage in physical self-care.

- **Practice experiencing pleasure in your body.** This could be through sex, intimacy with another, or self-pleasure. If that feels too much, explore ways you can experience pleasure in your body that are not sexual. For example, taking a warm bath, brushing your hair, self-massage, or gua sha. Especially if you are a trauma survivor or have a marginalized identity, self-care and pleasure is crucial. As activist adrienne maree brown says in her book *Pleasure Activism*, "Pleasure is the point. Feeling good is not frivolous, it's freedom."[7]

- **Remember that this is a process.** There is always going to be more work to do on this as long as our culture continues to teach us that how we look determines our worth. Using these tools will help improve your body image, but for most of us, our body image will always be something we are contending with.

Chapter 14

Embracing the Journey

The best journeys are the ones that answer questions
that on the outset we never even thought to ask.

—Rick Ridgeway

"So, I have a wedding next weekend and I don't think I am going to be able to stay sober for it," Andrea tells me at the beginning of her session. We are meeting via video, as Andrea leaves for Peru tomorrow. I can see her large suitcase is already neatly packed in the corner.

"You don't want to or don't think you'll be able to?"

"Don't think I'll be able to," Andrea says nervously. "It's my cousin's wedding and my whole extended family is going to be there."

"Families can be really tough," I say.

"Yeah, and there's this pretty big expectation that you should drink together. Peruvians are really serious about their beer traditions."

"Well, I think telling your family before you go to the wedding is going to be easier than doing it in the moment."

"Yeah, it just feels like such a big deal to bring it up beforehand. I don't want to have a whole conversation about it. I don't even know if I want to stop drinking after the ninety-day mark."

"I understand that, and you can absolutely choose to not continue with this experiment. But I also think this is a big opportunity for growth if you want it.... A way to really step out of the mold of people pleasing your family and say no."

"Yeah ... I also just don't want to drink when I'm there. It's stressful enough without being worried I am going to drink too much and cause a fight." Andrea sighs.

"And you have been practicing saying no and setting boundaries. You've done it with your classmates."

"Yeah, my family just feels so much more overwhelming. They just care so much about what other people think. I don't think my parents actually care, but they will probably be worried that my cousin will think it's disrespectful or something."

"People pleasing tends to get passed down. Most people pleasers start out as parent pleasers. What if this is your chance to break that cycle?"

Andrea smiles ... "Okay."

Dealing with Your Family

Depending on your relationship with your family, telling them may be even more difficult than telling your friends that you are questioning your relationship with alcohol. While friends may pressure you to drink because they want to continue to go out and party with you or because they feel self-conscious about their own drinking, your family is more likely to take your sobriety personally. Parents especially are more likely to feel responsible for your choices or feel like your life is a reflection of them. They may worry about the stigma of sobriety. I know a few of the questions my parents asked me were "Aren't you going to isolate yourself from your friends?!" "How will you ever date or get married if you can't drink?!" They may feel embarrassed and say things like "Okay but don't tell your Aunt Sue, she's old and won't understand!" . . . to which I want to remind you that *you* have a right to choose who and when you tell. Maybe you don't want to tell your Aunt Sue, maybe you want to tell as few people as possible because you aren't sure about your future relationship with alcohol, so you don't care, or maybe hiding this piece of yourself feels like lying. This is something only you can figure out. You have a right to say, "I appreciate your concern. While Aunt Sue may not understand, I don't feel comfortable hiding this piece of myself. I want to be honest with her regardless of her reaction."

Older family members can also feel like they know you better than you know yourself because they still think of you as a child. Your family may also have concerns that you are overreacting when you tell them you are going to stop drinking. They may say, "Come on, you weren't that bad!" Or "Why don't you just try cutting back?" But keep in mind, they may not be the best judge of your relationship with alcohol. Do they have a healthy relationship with alcohol themselves? Do they know how much you were drinking or partying? Have they seen all the times you got kicked out of the bar? Or spent the whole Sunday in bed hungover with sky-high anxiety? You don't need to justify your decision. This is your life, and you get to decide what works and doesn't work for you. You also don't need people to agree with or like your decision to stop drinking in order to respect your boundaries.

Is Moderation Possible?

"It's officially been over ninety days. I didn't drink at the wedding," Andrea says as she plops down on my couch.

"Congratulations!" I say, "that's a big deal. How are you feeling?"

"Good! I feel like I learned a lot and am proud of myself for doing this. But I am just ready to try to drink moderately. I feel like I've had a good break from it, and I think with these new tools I will be able to drink less."

While I have some slight concerns about Andrea drinking again, I do think it's crucially important that everyone decide for themselves if they want to stop drinking. Sometimes that looks like stopping for a period of time and trying to drink again. It may look like experimenting. Sometimes we have to see for ourselves if we are able to do it or not. Everyone is different, and for some folks the costs of not drinking may outweigh the benefits, depending on what is going on in their life, their values, and their goals. This can also change over time. So, if you have read this far in the book and are not quite convinced total sobriety is for you, no problem! Let's talk about moderation and what the research says.

Many people who come to see me share that the goal for them is not to quit drinking entirely but to drink less and avoid the consequences of drinking too much. I do know some people who do it successfully, but statistically, it is much easier to quit drinking altogether than to successfully moderate. Remember, unlike food or sugar, alcohol is an *addictive substance*. Therefore, moderation of something chemically addictive is going to inherently be difficult, especially if you have a history of overusing it.

One reason why moderation is difficult is because it requires you to be constantly making decisions. Am I going to drink today? When? How much? What am I going to drink? Should I have another? According to social psychologist Roy F. Baumeister, decision fatigue is the emotional or mental exhaustion that occurs when you are continuously weighing your options and making choices.[1] According to his research, the more decisions you make in a day, even if they are small and mundane, the more exhausted you get and the more likely you are to make a poor choice. This is why it is so much easier to not drink.

You make one decision, and stick with that versus constantly making lots of little decisions and trying to ensure you don't drink too much. It's also a double whammy in this case. Not only do you get decision fatigue from moderating, but when you do have a drink, the alcohol impairs your ability to think rationally and carefully weigh your options. These factors together make it much harder to moderate and not fall back into old patterns.

The longer you have been drinking and trying to change your drinking habits will also determine how difficult moderation is for you. This is because your brain literally changes when a habit is created. As neuroscientist Marc Lewis discusses in *The Biology of Desire*, "Brain change equals synaptic modification, and synaptic modification results from synaptic activity that is boosted by emotion, attention and repetition. . . . Cells that fire [together] . . . end up being more strongly connected."[2] To put this more simply, the more your brain repeats a particular pattern, the deeper the pathway of this pattern is ingrained. Think about bike tire tracks in mud. The first few times, it can be difficult to ride, but eventually if you keep taking the same path over and over, it is going to be such a deep groove it will be difficult to ride down the path without using the preexisting tracks. However, if you start forming new habits, and create a new track next to the preexisting one, the older pattern does not just disappear.[3] It does not get any deeper because you aren't using it, but it doesn't go away. Even if you develop a new habit, the old habit groove will be waiting for you, ready to pick right back up where you left off. This is part of the reason why drinkers can have success moderating or being abstinent and then, all of the sudden, get triggered and fall back into an old pattern and end up drinking just as much as they were before. Your brain does not just have a "reset button" when it comes to habits.

According to habit researcher Charles Duhigg, habits consist of three parts: cue, routine, and reward; together these create a habit loop.[4] The cue is a specific trigger—whether this is the time of day, an emotion, or a location—that causes us to crave a specific reward. For example, we wake up in the morning, taste our morning breath, and crave the minty taste of our toothpaste, prompting us to brush our teeth. Habits stick because we crave the reward. If we can crave the taste of toothpaste, can you imagine how much more difficult a habit is to break when we are craving an artificially pleasurable substance like alcohol, which if you remember from Chapter 5 also causes us to need more over time to experience the same effect (unlike toothpaste!).

Drinking alcohol is not just a habit. According to research by psychologists Kent Berridge and Terry Robinson, over time, individuals who use drugs or alcohol become hypersensitive to these cues that form habits.[5] According to their incentive-sensitization theory, this causes "excessive amplification specifically of psychological 'wanting,' especially triggered by cues, without necessarily an amplification of 'liking.'"[6] This means that over time, drinkers become hypersensitive to cues (this could be the smell of alcohol, the experience of stress, or seeing the time is 5 p.m.) and increasingly crave or want the reward of alcohol, even though they do not like drinking more. Oftentimes, they actually like drinking less because their tolerance grows, and they need more to experience the same effect. Furthermore, this theory states that this hypersensitivity and affinity for the substance doesn't ever go away, even after a period of abstinence. This means that even after you take a break from alcohol, your brain will react with the same strong desire to drink as when you were at the height of your drinking.[7] Taking a break may reset your tolerance, but it will not change how your brain has learned it should consume alcohol.

So why do I recommend then that you take a break from drinking for at least thirty days if we aren't resetting your brain? You may not be able to change your old wiring and habits in your brain, but you can create new habits. These won't rid you of your old habits, but they will give you a shot at being able to do something different. For example, you start to change your brain every time you call a friend or take a hot bath to deal with your stress instead of drinking. You start to change your brain when you practice meeting friends or going on dates sober instead of relying on alcohol to deal with your nerves. While practicing these new habits for thirty days will not be the same deeply formed habits as years of drinking, it will give you a chance to do something different and choose a new path. It's important to note that it is much easier to chart a *new path* that hasn't been worn than try to change a worn, deep old path. To give you a visual, imagine how hard it would be to start down the well-trodden bike path and then ride right next to it, without falling back into the old groove for a period of time. This is what it is like to try to moderate your drinking. For most of us, it is actually much easier to just stop drinking altogether.

Below is a list of experiences that make moderating more difficult. The more that apply to you the more difficult it will be for you to moderate your alcohol intake.

- If you have been physically addicted to alcohol
- The length of time you've been drinking this way. The longer it's been, the harder it will be to moderate.
- If you are drinking daily
- If your drinking has a specific ritual, for example, making your own mixed drink at night, drinking at the same time every day, frequenting the same bar, drinking every Friday, or using alcohol as a reward for getting through something
- If you rarely drink without getting drunk—or don't see the point of this
- If you have felt as though alcohol is the "solution" to your problems or worries

- If you use alcohol to deal with stress
- If you use alcohol to deal with social anxiety
- If you have a history of trauma, PTSD, anxiety, or other mental health issues
- If you have a history of self-sabotage and don't trust yourself when you say you will do something

Tips for Mindful Drinking

If you do decide to try moderating, my recommendation is to abstain from alcohol for at least thirty days. Often, people may try to start moderating right away, or they want to quit drinking for a week and they start drinking again before any of the positive effects of sobriety kick in. Set a small, reasonable goal. If thirty days is too long, start with ten and go from there. Don't think about the idea of forever. It can be so overwhelming and is a completely fruitless exercise that only helps us justify continuing to drink. If thirty days goes well, see if you can do another thirty. Maybe another. There is a legitimate reason why AA talks about taking things one day at a time. You don't have to make a plan for the rest of your life. You can experiment and see what works for you. Typically, the cravings from alcohol, mental or physical, decrease dramatically after ninety days. By then, your new habits will be in full swing and you will be able to get a real taste for what sobriety feels like. Remember to treat yourself **very kindly** during this time. Be sure to engage in basic self-care: food, water, rest, sunlight, sleep. Keep your to-do list to bare necessities. Everything beyond this and not drinking is extra credit.

This break from alcohol will also give you enough time to take note of your triggers and common patterns of drinking so you can create new ones. There are four major types of triggers, though some of them overlap. For some of these triggers, we know in advance if we are going to experience them. We know a family gathering will be stressful so we can prepare or decline the invitation. However, some of these triggers will be unexpected. Someone offers you a bottle of champagne because you got promoted, or you run into an old drinking buddy. In both cases, understanding your triggers and making a plan for what you will do in the event that this happens is vitally important whether you want to moderate your drinking or stop altogether.

Emotional triggers refer to our desire to drink as a result of our emotions or stress. Almost all of us have experiences of turning to alcohol in order to numb or regulate our emotions. However, it's important to understand which emotions are most triggering for you. For some it may be anger while for others it is sadness or loneliness. Use this break to get clear on what your emotional triggers are and refer back to Chapter 8 to implement the skills we discussed in order to regulate your emotions without alcohol.

Environmental triggers refer to when our environment creates a desire to drink. An environmental trigger could be a place you used to drink at, like a bar or the office, or even a room in your house. It could also be any sights, smells, or sounds that may trigger you. For example, a whiff of orange juice reminds you of all the screwdrivers you used to consume, or you hear a song that reminds you of your nights at a certain club. Environmental triggers can also include people that you may want to avoid, like your friend that you only frequent a bar with, or seeing your ex, which makes you nervous and want a drink.

Exposure triggers refer to when seeing alcohol or other's drinking causes us to desire to drink. This could look like seeing people drink at a family party, watching someone whip out a flask at a meeting, being offered a drink on a plane, watching someone get drunk on TV, or finding a bottle of wine you didn't know you had in your basement.

Temporal triggers refer to when certain times of day or year or holidays cause us to desire to drink. This could be as simple as the clock striking 5 p.m., signaling the day is over and you want to make your usual drink, wanting to celebrate your birthday by popping champagne, or really wanting Grandma's eggnog at a holiday gathering.

Exercise:

Throughout the next thirty days, make a list of your emotional, environmental, exposure, and temporal triggers. Most exposure triggers will be unexpected; however, you can guess based on your lifestyle which ones you may experience, or which ones would be the most triggering for you. Complete the sentence: "If ____ (the trigger), I will ____." Make a plan for what you will do to take care of yourself, whom you can call, or how you will remove yourself from the situation if needed.

Example: Emotional Trigger

"If I feel lonely and want to drink, I will call my friend and snuggle with my pet."

Example: Environmental Trigger

"If I get a craving for a drink after work, I will make myself a mocktail."

Example: Exposure Trigger

"If someone offers me a shot, I will say no and go to the bathroom to remove myself from the situation and take a break. I can go home early if I need to."

Example: Temporal Trigger

"If I get a craving to drink on my birthday, I will organize a birthday outing with my friends where alcohol isn't served."

If you choose to moderate, my recommendation is to only drink if it is **planned at least twenty-four hours in advance.** This will ensure you are drinking because you want to rather than drinking in response to a trigger, whether it is conscious or not. As Roy Baumeister says, "The best decision makers are the ones who know when *not* to trust themselves."[8] Do not trust your knee-jerk reaction to a trigger. Wait twenty-four hours to see if you really want that drink. I also recommend not using alcohol to deal with your emotions. In Chapter 8, we talked about how it is ineffective for processing your emotions. An additional fact is that when you are in an emotional state, it is going to be even more difficult to moderate. If you decide to drink, plan it out and make it a deliberate choice. Allow yourself to savor the experience and be mindful of how you feel before, during, and after. Ask yourself, "Was this worth it?" Maybe it is, maybe it isn't. Could a mocktail do the trick instead? Only you will know. As Holly Whitaker says, sometimes, we don't actually want a drink, we want a "moment."[9] We want a time where we can shut off our brain, pause, and maybe experience a little indulgence. I find that a moment can be created with a cup of tea, a mocktail, sitting outside and taking a deep breath, or going someplace where alcohol isn't served or eating a piece of chocolate.

Working Through Relapse and Slipups

It is very common throughout this process to not meet your goals completely on the first try. When people relapse or slip up, they often feel the need to beat themselves up and call themselves names, aka shame themselves. They think that they must punish themselves in order to atone for what they've done, as if the crueler they are, the less likely they will be to do it again. This is completely false. When you beat yourself up, you are literally stressing yourself out. And what do most of us drinkers want to do when we experience stress? You guessed it, drink! So, when you beat yourself up for drinking too much, you are literally triggering yourself to drink more. **Please do not do this.** Even if you don't believe you deserve it, know that treating yourself kindly actually makes it easier to change and achieve your goals. In Kristin Neff's book, *Self-Compassion: The Proven Power of Being Kind to Yourself*, she outlines the three elements of self-compassion.[10]

1. **Self-Kindness vs. Self-Judgment**, which looks like treating and talking to yourself as you would a friend or a child. Being kind toward yourself and tending to yourself rather than judging, criticizing, or punishing yourself.
2. **Common Humanity vs. Isolation**, which looks like recognizing that you are a fallible, imperfect human being. Remind yourself that all human beings struggle, and you are not alone in how you feel.
3. **Mindfulness vs. Over-Identification**, which looks like practicing mindfulness and nonjudgmentally noticing how you feel. Remember, you are not your thoughts. Check back to Chapter 7 for exercises on how to defuse your thoughts.

Self-compassion is not resignation. It does not mean that you give up on important things that matter to you or that you allow yourself to do whatever you want whenever you want. As I told Andrea, you can whip the donkey to get it to move forward quickly, or you can move the donkey forward with a carrot and praise. The latter may take longer, but it will create enduring change based on trust instead of fear. In order to create real change with yourself, you must be compassionate to yourself while also holding yourself accountable. Just as we discussed in Chapter 10 that you can be compassionate to others *and* set boundaries with them, you can do the same for yourself.

How do we do this? Start by honestly yet nonjudgmentally assessing if a certain action or behavior is working. If you continue to slip up, I invite you to ask yourself, "Is moderating working for me?" If the answer is no, what are some different things you can try? Use the costs and payoffs exercise (page 68–69) to determine if moderating is really working for you long term. Give yourself room to experiment and try different things before shaming yourself or giving up. One of the most common things that stops people from continuing on the path to exploring sobriety is shame and perfectionism. They decide that because they have relapsed a few times, they are a hopeless case.

As a therapist, I don't believe in hopeless cases. I believe most human beings are so much more powerful and capable than they think they are. One of the greatest joys of my life is watching people delightfully surprise me with their ability to change and grow. Right when I start to give up hope is often when the miracles happen.

Never in my life did I believe that I would write a book, let alone one about sobriety. It was something I felt shame about for a long time. I used to think something was wrong with me because I couldn't "drink like everyone else." I used to show up to dates early and order a club soda and pretend I was drinking because I believed I would never be able to find a partner if they knew I was sober. Now, I know that being sober is actually my superpower. It is truly the greatest decision I have ever made. It has been an anchor in my life that has allowed me to live the most honest, courageous, and deeply fulfilling life possible. One that is not easy, simple, or free of struggle, but one that is beautiful; one that I have designed on my own. I have a sense of unshakeable self-worth that I never thought would be possible. I am amazed at how sobriety has transformed the lives of others and given them the same miraculous but completely unique results.

Regardless of which path you choose, I wish you a wonderful life. You deserve a life that is free from constantly worrying and beating yourself up about alcohol or any other coping skill that hurts you long term. I used to think freedom meant being free from accountability; I relished being free to do whatever I wanted and not answering to anyone. Rebellion felt like freedom. So, the idea of abstaining from alcohol for the rest of my life seemed like bondage. Now, I know that true freedom involves creating a life that you don't need to escape from. One where you don't have to tolerate a problematic pattern in your life just because everyone else does. True freedom is when you create your own life based on your values, desires, and needs rather than living based on other people's lives or expectations. You deserve to live a life that is free from the bondage of drinking and shame. You deserve to live a life that you will look back on and be deeply proud of. Regardless of what that looks like or where you end up, I hope this book makes a difference for you. May this be just the beginning.

Resources

Sobriety Instagram Pages and Online Sober Communities

@asobergirlsguide
@counterculture_club
@joinclubsoda
@joinmonument
@jointempest
@1000hoursdry
@proudandsober
@recoveryfortherevolution
@reframe_app
@sans_bar
@servedupsober
@sherecovers

@soberbabesclub
@soberblackgirlsclub
@soberbrowngirls
@sobergirlssociety
@soberirl
@sobermomsquad
@sobervoices
@sherecovers
@theluckiestclub
@theretiredpartygirl
@thesoberkates
@thisnakedmind

Books on Sobriety

Drink: The Intimate Relationship Between Women and Alcohol by Ann Dowsett Johnston

Drinking: A Love Story by Caroline Knapp

Mindful Drinking: How Cutting Down Can Change Your Life by Rosamund Dean

Quit Like a Woman: The Radical Choice to Not Drink in a Culture Obsessed with Alcohol by Holly Whitaker

Sober Curious: The Blissful Sleep, Greater Focus, and Deep Connection Awaiting Us All on the Other Side of Alcohol by Ruby Warrington

The Sober Girl Society Handbook: An Empowering Guide to Living Hangover Free by Millie Gooch

The Sober Lush: A Hedonist's Guide to Living a Decadent, Adventurous, Soulful Life—Alcohol Free by Amanda Eyre Ward and Jardine Libaire

This Naked Mind: Control Alcohol, Find Freedom, Rediscover Happiness & Change Your Life by Annie Grace

The Unexpected Joy of Being Sober by Catherine Gray
We Are the Luckiest: The Surprising Magic of a Sober Life by Laura McKowen

Podcasts on Sobriety

The After Party with The Sober Kates
Home Podcast
In Recovery
This Naked Mind with Annie Grace
Recovery Happy Hour
Recovery Rocks
Seltzer Squad
Sober as a Mother
Sober Curious with Ruby Warrington
Sober Sex

Sober Bars

Bar Tonique in New Orleans, LA
The Edge Sober Bar in Willow Hill, IL
Getaway in New York, NY
Listen Bar in New York, NY
The Other Side in Crystal Lake, IL
Sans Bar in Austin, TX
27 Restaurant & Bar in Miami, FL
Vena's Fizz House in Portland, ME

Books on Privilege and How It Impacts Mental Health

Citizens but Not Americans: Race and Belonging Among Latino Millennials by Nilda
    Flores-González
Gender Outlaw: On Men, Women, and the Rest of Us by Kate Bornstein
Hood Feminism: Notes from the Women a Movement Forgot by Mikki Kendall
I'm Still Here: Black Dignity in a World Made for Whiteness by Austin Channing
    Brown
Minor Feelings: An Asian American Reckoning by Cathy Park Hong
*My Grandmother's Hands: Racialized Trauma and the Pathway to Mending Our
    Hearts and Bodies* by Ressma Menakem
*Radical Belonging: How to Survive and Thrive in an Unjust World (While Trans-
    forming It for the Better)* by Lindo Bacon
Sister Outsider by Audre Lorde

So You Want to Talk About Race by Ijeoma Oluo

What We Don't Talk About When We Talk About Fat by Aubrey Gordon

You Are Your Best Thing: Vulnerability, Shame Resilience, and the Black Experience by Tarana Burke

Books on Eating Disorder Recovery, Body Positivity, and Diet Culture

Anti-Diet: Reclaim Your Time, Money, Well-Being, and Happiness Through Intuitive Eating by Christy Harrison

The Body Is Not an Apology: The Power of Radical Self-Love by Sonya Renee Taylor

Body Respect: What Conventional Health Books Get Wrong, Leave Out and Just Plain Fail to Understand About Weight by Lindo Bacon and Lucy Aphramor

The Diet-Free Revolution: 10 Steps to Free Yourself from the Diet Cycle with Mindful Eating and Radical Self-Acceptance by Alexis Conason

Fearing the Black Body: The Racial Origins of Fatphobia by Sabrina Strings

Food Isn't Medicine by Dr. Joshua Wolrich

The Fuck It Diet: Eating Should Be Easy by Caroline Dooner

Intuitive Eating: A Revolutionary Anti-Diet Approach by Elyse Resch and Evelyn Tribole

Just Eat It: How Intuitive Eating Can Help You Get Your Shit Together Around Food by Laura Thompson

More Than a Body: Your Body Is an Instrument, Not an Ornament by Lindsay and Lexie Kite

Train Happy: An Intuitive Exercise Plan for Every Body by Tally Rye

Unapologetic Eating: Make Peace with Food and Transform Your Life by Alissa Rumsey

You Have the Right to Remain Fat by Virgie Tovar

Instagram Pages on Eating Disorder Recovery, Body Positivity, Diet Culture

@beauty_redefined

@blackandembodied

@bodyimage_therapist

@bodyimagewithbri

@bodyposipanda

@bodypositive_dietician

@dieticiananna

@evelyntribole

@iamchrissyking

@sonyareneetaylor

@theantidietplan

@thefuckitdiet

@thenutritiontea

@thethicknutritionist

@tiffanyima

@your.latina.nutritionist

Therapy Directories

Asian Mental Health Collective (www.asianmhc.org)
Brainspotting Therapists (www.brainspotting.com/directory)
EMDR International Association (www.emdria.org/find-a-therapist)
Inclusive Therapists (www.inclusivetherapists.com)
Latinx Therapy (www.latinxtherapy.com)
Melanin and Mental Health (www.melaninandmentalhealth.com)
Monarch (www.meetmonarch.com)
Open Path Collective—Reduced Rate Therapy (www.openpathcollective.org)
Psychology Today (www.psychologytoday.com)
Therapy Den (www.therapyden.com)
Therapy for Black Girls (therapyforblackgirls.com)
Theravive (www.theravive.com)

Acknowledgments

I need to start out by thanking everyone who paved the way for this book to happen. This book was possible because of other people's research, guts, and knowledge that all came before me. To the trailblazers in the field of normalizing sobriety and questioning your relationship with alcohol, such as Annie Grace, Holly Whitaker, Catherine Gray, Ruby Warrington, Laura McKowen, and so many more, I am deeply indebted to you. To Brené Brown and Glennon Doyle, thank you for your willingness to share about your sobriety. Your work inspired me when I was in the depths of my addiction and was a light that guided me out.

To all the activists, eating disorder therapists, researchers, and dieticians, thank you for all your work to go against the grain so that I was able to connect the dots between diet and alcohol culture. I want to thank all the fat activists and individuals in marginalized bodies, especially the Black, Indigenous, and People of Color who so often are not properly credited and acknowledged for their contributions. To Sonya Renee Taylor, Sabrina Strings, and Aubrey Gordon, thank you for your writing, and to all the amazing activists on Instagram who tirelessly put out content and education for free, this book would not be the same without you.

To all my Instagram followers, who have trusted me, called me out, and pushed me to be a better version of myself, thank you for all your support. To all the Instagram therapists, whom I have learned from and grown with so much over the years, especially Lisa Olivera (who introduced me to her amazing agent), Whitney Goodman, Hayden Dawes, and Elizabeth Earnshaw, it's an honor to be your peer in this field.

To my husband, who bore the brunt of the emotional coaster that is writing a book, you are my favorite person in the world. I would never have been able to write this book without you holding down the fort, taking care of everything, and understanding when I went into crazy, not-sleeping writing mode.

To my parents, who enthusiastically read every version of this book and gave me their feedback even with extremely quick turnarounds, you are my biggest cheerleaders, and I am so lucky to have you in my life. I would not be sober today without your support. To my brother, Kevin, who read the book early, and to my friends who supported me throughout this whole journey and never questioned that it would be possible, Ashley, Liz, Lex, Eli, and Aly, I love you so much.

To my amazing agent, Laura Lee Mattingly, who took a chance on me, was able to take my messy vision and help me translate it into this book, and came up with the amazing title when I couldn't think of anything, thank you from the bottom of my heart. I love working with you.

Thank you to the whole team at Hachette Go who brought this book into the world, especially my editors, Renee Sedliar and Alison Dalafave, whose insight and recommendations made this book the absolute best version it could be.

Notes

Introduction

1. @sobergirlsociety, quote from Millie Gooch (@milliegooch), Instagram, May 14, 2020, https://www.instagram.com/p/CAKlsCEg7z-/?igshid=15yyixtx7io0s.

Chapter 1

1. The Big Book of Alcoholics Anonymous (AA's textbook) was first published in 1939 and revised in 1955 to include women. Revisions in 1976 and 2001 added more stories and updated statistics.

2. Annie Grace, *This Naked Mind: Control Alcohol, Find Freedom, Discover Happiness, & Change Your Life* (New York, NY: Avery, 2019).

Chapter 2

1. Russ Harris, *The Happiness Trap: How to Stop Struggling and Start Living* (Boston, MA: Trumpeter Books, 2008).

2. Robin Dunbar, a notable professor of psychology at University of Oxford, studied the correlation between social primates' brain sizes and the number of members in their clan. He has proven that the largest number of primates or people that can exist in a clan is 150 people.

3. Sarah L. Canham, Pia M. Mauro, Christopher N. Kaufmann, and Andrew Sixsmith, "Association of Alcohol Use and Loneliness Frequency Among Middle-Aged and Older Adult Drinkers," *Journal of Aging and Health* 28, no. 2 (2016): 267–284, https://doi.org/10.1177/0898264315589579.

4. Viviana E. Horigian, Renae D. Schmidt, and Daniel J. Feaster, "Loneliness, Mental Health, and Substance Use Among US Young Adults During COVID-19," *Journal of Psychoactive Drugs* 53, no. 1 (2021): 1–9, doi: 10.1080/02791072.2020.1836435.

5. David Ducharme, "COVID-19 Is Making America's Loneliness Epidemic Even Worse," *Time Magazine*, May 8, 2020.

6. Yuval Noah Harari, *Sapiens: A Brief History of Humankind* (New York: Harper Perennial, 2018).

7. Ibid.

8. Emily Nagoski and Amelia Nagoski, *Burnout: The Secret to Unlocking the Stress Cycle* (New York, NY: Ballantine, 2019).

9. Elizabeth Stanley, *Widen the Window: Training Your Brain and Body to Thrive During Stress and Recover from Trauma* (New York, NY: Avery, 2019).

10. Nagoski and Nagoski, *Burnout.*

11. Robert Sapolsky, *Why Zebras Don't Get Ulcers: The Acclaimed Guide to Stress-Related Diseases and Coping* (New York, NY: Holt Paperbacks, 2004).

Chapter 3

1. The idea that stress and trauma are on the same continuum is credited to Elizabeth Stanley and discussed in her in book *Widen the Window: Training Your Brain and Body to Thrive During Stress and Recover from Trauma* (New York, NY: Avery, 2019).

2. Bruce Duncan Perry and Maia Szalavitz, *The Boy Who Was Raised as a Dog: And Other Stories from a Child Psychiatrist's Notebook: What Traumatized Children Can Teach Us About Loss, Love, and Healing* (New York, NY: Basic Books, 2017).

3. Martin E. Seligman, Robert A. Rosellini, and Michael J. Kozak, "Learned Helplessness in the Rat: Time Course, Immunization, and Reversibility," *Journal of Comparative and Physiological Psychology* 88, no. 2 (1975): 542–547, https://doi.org/10.1037/h0076431.

4. Perry and Szalavitz, *The Boy Who Was Raised as a Dog.*

5. Bessel van der Kolk, *The Body Keeps the Score: Brain, Mind, and Body in the Healing of Trauma* (New York, NY: Penguin Books, 2015).

6. Created by scientist Paul D. MacLean.

7. van der Kolk, *The Body Keeps the Score.*

8. Ibid.

Chapter 4

1. Taken from Macmillan Dictionary, https://www.macmillandictionary.com/us/dictionary/american/shame_1.

2. Brené Brown, *I Thought It Was Just Me (but It Isn't): Making the Journey from "What Will People Think?" to "I Am Enough"* (New York, NY: Avery, 2018).

3. Ibid.

4. Ibid.

5. Quoted in ibid.

6. "Alcohol Consumption Rises Sharply During Pandemic Shutdown; Heavy Drinking by Women Rises 41%," RAND Corporation, October 10, 2020, https://www.rand.org/news/press/2020/09/29.html.

7. Yuki Noguchi, "Sharp 'Off the Charts' Rise in Alcoholic Liver Disease Among Young Women," NPR, March 16, 2021, https://www.npr.org/sections /health-shots/2021/03/16/973684753/sharp-off-the-charts-rise-in-alcoholic-liver -disease-among-young-women.

8. van der Kolk, *The Body Keeps the Score.*

9. Brené Brown, *Daring Greatly: How the Courage to Be Vulnerable Transforms the Way We Live, Love, Parent, and Lead* (New York, NY: Avery, 2015).

10. Texas professor James Pennbaker studied rape and incest survivors and what happens when they kept their experiences a secret. Brené Brown cited this research in her book *Daring Greatly: How the Courage to Be Vulnerable Transforms the Way We Live, Love, Parent, and Lead* (New York, NY: Avery, 2015).

11. Bruce Duncan Perry and Maia Szalavitz, *The Boy Who Was Raised as a Dog: And Other Stories from a Child Psychiatrist's Notebook: What Traumatized Children Can Teach Us About Loss, Love, and Healing* (New York, NY: Basic Books, 2017).

12. Mark F. Schwartz, "Reenactments Related to Bonding and Hypersexuality," *Sexual Addiction & Compulsivity* 3, no. 3 (1996): 195–212, https://doi .org/10.1080/10720169608400112.

13. Antonia Abbey, "Alcohol-Related Sexual Assault: A Common Problem Among College Students," *Journal of Studies on Alcohol, Supplement* no. s14 (2002): 118–128, https://doi.org/10.15288/jsas.2002.s14.118.

Chapter 5

1. Rod Phillips, *Alcohol: A History* (Chapel Hill: University of North Carolina Press, 2014).

2. Ibid.

3. Holly Whitaker, *Quit Like a Woman: The Radical Choice to Not Drink in a Culture Obsessed with Alcohol* (New York, NY: Dial Press, 2019).

4. GBD 2016 Alcohol Collaborators, "Alcohol Use and Burden for 195 Countries and Territories, 1990–2016: A Systematic Analysis for the Global Burden of Disease Study 2016," *The Lancet* 392, no. 10152 (September 22, 2018): 1015–1035, https:// doi.org/https://doi.org/10.1016/S0140-6736(18)31310-2.

5. Samir Zahkari, "Overview: How Is Alcohol Metabolized by the Body?" *Alcohol Research & Health* 29, no. 4 (2006): 245–254.

6. Clair R. Martin, Vadim Osadchiy, Amir Kalani, and Emeran A. Mayer, "The Brain-Gut-Microbiome Axis," *Cellular and Molecular Gastroenterology and Hepatology* 6, no. 2 (2018): 133–148.

7. Jennifer L. Steiner, Kristen T. Crowell, and Charles H. Lang, "Impact of Alcohol on Glycemic Control and Insulin Action," *Biomolecules* 5, no. 4 (2015): 2223–2246.

8. Zahkari, "Overview: How Is Alcohol Metabolized by the Body?"

9. Helmut K. Seitz and Felix Stickel, "Acetaldehyde as an Underestimated Risk Factor for Cancer Development: Role of Genetics in Ethanol Metabolism," *Genes & Nutrition* 5, no. 2 (June 5, 2010): 121–128.

10. Rui Guo and Jun Ren, "Alcohol and Acetaldehyde in Public Health: From Marvel to Menace," *International Journal of Environmental Research and Public Health* 7, no. 4 (2010): 1285–1301, https://doi.org/10.3390/ijerph7041285.

11. Peter Boyle and Paolo Boffetta, "Alcohol Consumption and Breast Cancer Risk," *Breast Cancer Research* 11, S3 (2009), https://doi.org/10.1186/bcr 2422.

12. Matthew P. Walker, *Why We Sleep: The New Science of Sleep and Dreams* (New York, NY: Scribner, 2017).

13. Ibid.

14. Anya Topiwala et al., "No Safe Level of Alcohol Consumption for Brain Health: Observational Cohort Study of 25,378 UK Biobank Participants" (2021), unpublished manuscript of Nuffield Department Population Health, Big Data Institute, University of Oxford, Oxford, UK, https://www.medrxiv.org/content/10.110 1/2021.05.10.21256931v1.full.pdf.

15. Natalie Grover, "Any Amount of Alcohol Consumption Is Harmful to the Brain, Finds Study," *The Guardian,* May 18, 2021, https://www .theguardian.com/society/2021/may/18/any-amount-of-alcohol-consumption -harmful-to-the-brain-finds-study.

16. George F. Koob et al., "Addiction Is a Reward Deficit and Stress Surfeit Disorder," *Neuropharmacology* 76, part B (2014): 370–382.

17. Nora D. Volkow and Marisela Morales, "The Brain on Drugs: From Reward to Addiction," *Cell* 162, no. 4 (2015): 712–725, https://doi.org/10.1016/j .cell.2015.07.046.

18. Judith Grisel, *Never Enough: The Neuroscience and Experience of Addiction* (New York, NY: Anchor Books, 2018).

Chapter 6

1. From Merriam Webster Dictionary Online, https://www.merriam-webster .com/dictionary/consciousness.

Chapter 7

1. Russ Harris, *The Happiness Trap: How to Stop Struggling and Start Living* (Boston, MA: Trumpeter Books, 2008).

Chapter 8

1. Marc Brackett cited this statistic from his research on an *Unlocking Us* podcast with Brené Brown, https://brenebrown.com/podcast/dr-marc-brackett-and-brene-on-permission-to-feel/.

2. Lisa Feldman Barrett, *How Emotions Are Made: The Secret Life of the Brain* (Boston, MA: Houghton Mifflin Harcourt, 2017).

3. Ibid.

4. Marc A. Brackett, *Permission to Feel: Unlocking the Power of Emotions to Help Our Kids, Ourselves, and Our Society Thrive* (New York, NY: Celadon, 2019).

5. Ibid.

6. Feldman Barrett, *How Emotions Are Made.*

7. Jonathan Posner, James A. Russell, and Bradley S. Peterson, "The Circumplex Model of Affect: An Integrative Approach to Affective Neuroscience, Cognitive Development, and Psychopathology," *Development and Psychopathology* 17, no. 3 (2005): 715–734, https://doi.org/10.1017/s0954579405050340.

8. Feldman Barrett, *How Emotions Are Made.*

9. David Robson, "There Really Are 50 Eskimo Words for 'Snow,'" *Washington Post*, January 14, 2013.

10. Sabrina Stierwalt, "Why Do We Laugh?" *Scientific American*, February 9, 2020, https://www.scientificamerican.com/article/why-do-we-laugh/.

11. Jane Brody, "Biological Role of Emotional Tears," *New York Times*, August 31, 1982.

Chapter 9

1. Todd Bridgman, Stephen Cummings, and John Ballard, "Who Built Maslow's Pyramid? A History of the Creation of Management Studies' Most Famous Symbol and Its Implications for Management Education," *Academy of Management Learning & Education* 18, no. 1 (2019): 81–98, https://journals.aom.org/doi/abs/10.5465/amle.2017.0351.

2. Scott Barry Kaufman, *Transcend: The New Science of Self-Actualization* (New York, NY: Penguin Books, 2021).

3. Ibid.

4. Ibid.

5. Harry Harlow, "The Nature of Love" *American Psychologist* 13, no. 12 (1958): 673–685, doi:10.1037/h0047884.

6. Barry Kaufman, *Transcend.*

Chapter 10

1. Brené Brown, *Dare to Lead: Brave Work, Tough Conversations, Whole Hearts* (New York, NY: Random House, 2018).

2. Mark Groves, "Self-Love, WTF Does That Even Mean?!," *Create the Love* (blog), https://createthelove.com/self-love-wtf-does-that-even-mean/.

Chapter 11

1. Kimberlé Williams Crenshaw, "Mapping the Margins: Intersectionality, Identity Politics, and Violence Against Women of Color," in *The Public Nature of Private Violence*, eds. Martha Albertson Fineman and Roxanne Mykitiuk (New York: Routledge, 1994), 93–118.

2. Christy Harrison, *Anti-Diet: Reclaim Your Time, Money, Well-Being, and Happiness Through Intuitive Eating* (New York, NY: Little Brown Spark, 2019).

3. Alison Fildes et al., "Probability of an Obese Person Attaining Normal Body Weight: Cohort Study Using Electronic Health Records," *American Journal of Public Health* 105, no. 9 (2015): 54–59, https://doi.org/10.2105/ajph.2015.30 2773.

4. Christy Harrison cites Traci Mann et al., "Medicare's Search for Effective Obesity Treatments: Diets Are Not the Answer," *American Psychologist* 62, no. 3 (April 2007): 220–233.

5. "The $72 Billion Weight Loss and Diet Control Market in the United States, 2019–2023—Why Meal Replacements Are Still Booming, but Not OTC Diet Pills—ResearchAndMarkets.com," AP NEWS, Associated Press, February 25, 2019, https://apnews.com/ec35f3315f9a4816985615391f41815a.

6. Sabrina Strings, *Fearing the Black Body: The Racial Origins of Fat Phobia* (New York, NY: NYU Press, 2019).

7. Sissi Cao, Rahim Moineddin, Marcelo L. Urquia, Fahad Razak, and Joel G. Ray, "J-Shapedness: An Often Missed, Often Miscalculated Relation: The Example of Weight and Mortality," *Journal of Epidemiology and Community Health* 68, no. 7 (2014): 683–690, https://doi.org/10.1136/jech-2013-203439.

8. Linda Bacon and Lucy Aphramor, "Weight Science: Evaluating the Evidence for a Paradigm Shift," *Nutrition Journal* 10, no. 1 (2011), https://doi.org/10.1186/1475-2891-10-9.

9. Erin N. Harrop and G. Alan Marlatt, "The Comorbidity of Substance Use Disorders and Eating Disorders in Women: Prevalence, Etiology, and Treatment," *Addictive Behaviors* 35, no. 5 (2010): 392–398, https://doi.org/10.1016/j.addbeh.2009.12.016.

10. Crescent B. Martin et al., "Attempts to Lose Weight Among Adults in the United States, 2013–2016," Centers for Disease Control and Prevention (NCHS Data Brief No. 313, July 18, 2018), https://www.cdc.gov/nchs/data/databriefs/db313.pdf.

11. Margaret L. Westwater, Paul C. Fletcher, and Hisham Ziauddeen, "Sugar Addiction: The State of the Science," *European Journal of Nutrition* 55, no. S2 (February 2016): 55–69, https://doi.org/10.1007/s00394-016-1229-6.

12. Harrison, *Anti-Diet.*

13. Daniela Coppola, "Total Alcoholic Beverage Sales in the U.S. 2006–2019," Statista, November 30, 2020, https://www.statista.com.

Chapter 12

1. "Youth Risk Behavior Surveillance System (YRBSS) 2019," Centers for Disease Control and Prevention, https://www.cdc.gov/healthyyouth/data/yrbs/index.htm.

2. "Fall Semester—a Time for Parents to Discuss the Risks of College Drinking," National Institute on Alcohol Abuse and Alcoholism, US Department of Health and Human Services, August 2020, https://www.niaaa.nih.gov/publications/brochures-and-fact-sheets/time-for-parents-discuss-risks-college-drinking.

3. Susan Cain, *Quiet: The Power of Introverts in a World That Can't Stop Talking* (New York, NY: Random House, 2013).

4. Ibid.

5. Ibid.

6. Lisa Held, "Psychoanalysis Shapes Consumer Culture," *Monitor on Psychology* 40, no. 11 (2009), https://doi.org/10.1037/e616502009-017.

7. Edward Bernays, "The Engineering of Consent," *ANNALS of the American Academy of Political and Social Science* 250, no. 1 (March 1, 1947): 113–120, https://doi.org/10.1177/000271624725000116.

8. Holly Whitaker, *Quit Like a Woman: The Radical Choice to Not Drink in a Culture Obsessed with Alcohol* (New York, NY: Dial Press, 2019).

9. Catherine Gray, *The Unexpected Joy of Being Sober* (London, UK: Octopus Publishing Group, 2017).

Chapter 13

1. Definition from Lexico.com, a collaboration between Dictionary.com and Oxford University Press, https://www.lexico.com/en/definition/inhibition.

2. "The Myth of Beer Goggles?" *Discover Magazine*, August 20, 2015, https://www.discovermagazine.com/mind/the-myth-of-beer-goggles.

3. William H. George et al., "Women's Sexual Arousal: Effects of High Alcohol Dosages and Self-Control Instructions," *Hormones and Behavior* 59, no. 5 (March 23, 2011): 730–738, https://doi.org/10.1016/j.yhbeh.2011.03.006.

4. Lexie Kite and Lindsay Kite, *More Than a Body: Your Body Is an Instrument, Not an Ornament* (Boston, MA: Houghton Mifflin Harcourt, 2021).

5. Emily Nagoski, *Come as You Are: The Surprising New Science That Will Transform Your Sex Life* (New York, NY: Simon & Schuster Paperbacks, 2021).

6. Ibid.

7. adrienne maree brown, *Pleasure Activism: The Politics of Feeling Good* (Chico, CA: AK Press, 2019).

Chapter 14

1. Quoted in John Tierney, "Do You Suffer from Decision Fatigue," *New York Times*, August 17, 2011.

2. Marc D. Lewis, *The Biology of Desire: Why Addiction Is Not a Disease* (New York, NY: Public Affairs, 2018).

3. Ibid.

4. Charles Duhigg, *The Power of Habit: Why We Do What We Do in Life and Business* (New York, NY: Random House, 2014).

5. Kent C. Berridge and Terry E. Robinson, "Liking, Wanting, and the Incentive-Sensitization Theory of Addiction," *American Psychologist* 71, no. 8 (2016): 670–679, https://doi.org/10.1037/amp0000059.

6. Ibid.

7. Ibid.

8. Roy F. Baumeister and John Tierney, *Willpower: Rediscovering Our Greatest Strength* (London: Penguin, 2012).

9. Holly Whitaker, *Quit Like a Woman: The Radical Choice to Not Drink in a Culture Obsessed with Alcohol* (New York, NY: Dial Press, 2019).

10. Kristin Neff, *Self-Compassion: The Proven Power of Being Kind to Yourself* (New York, NY: HarperCollins, 2011).

Index